Allie M. Felker

Toyon

A book of holiday recitations for the children of the school, the home, and the church

Allie M. Felker
Toyon
A book of holiday recitations for the children of the school, the home, and the church
ISBN/EAN: 9783337290290

Printed in Europe, USA, Canada, Australia, Japan

Cover: Foto ©Paul-Georg Meister /pixelio.de

More available books at **www.hansebooks.com**

TOYON

A BOOK OF HOLIDAY RECITATIONS

FOR THE

Children of the School, the Home,
and the Church.

SELECTED AND ARRANGED BY

ALLIE M. FELKER.

THE WHITAKER & RAY COMPANY
(INCORPORATED)
SAN FRANCISCO, CAL.
1899

TOYON.

Welcome, holly-berries,
   In Christmas canyons grown!
Friends in California,
   Hang up the red toyon!
Wreathe your halls and windows,
   Let Christmas cheer be known!
Friends in California,
   Hang up the red toyon!

Dedication.

To L. M. W., R. F. E., and the children of California this book is lovingly dedicated.

—*A. M. F.*

PREFACE.

During the past ten years, I have received many letters from teachers asking me to give suggestions for holiday entertainments. Requests from little people are also constantly coming for "pieces" which they once recited. A number of these selections have been taken from *Primary Education* and *The Popular Educator*, and I am grateful to the Educational Publishing Company for permission to use them. I am also grateful to the New England Publishing Company for permission to publish selections which have appeared from time to time in the *American Primary Teacher* and the *Journal of Education*. To *Intelligence*, the *Western Journal of Education* and the *San Jose Mercury*, thanks are also due. To friends who have offered encouragement in the way of contributions and particularly to those who have assisted in revising manuscript, and preparing it for publication, I am deeply grateful.

The selections will speak for themselves. "The Seven Little Sisters," "Ten Little Indians," and "The Honolulu Children," are merely suggestive. That children may learn to love history, literature, and Nature in her varied aspects, the dramatic instinct must be cultivated. That they may understand people, they must imitate; that they may comprehend stories, they must dramatize; that they may develop true ideals, they must create.

Entertainments which are the result of actual school work—those developed by the pupils under the direction of a live teacher—are educational in character. I trust that the selections in this book will prove helpful in working up such entertainments.

That a recognition of old friends in the following "pieces" may make them an unfailing source of pleasure to children, especially to little friends in California, is the wish of the one who sends them forth.

CONTENTS.

Christmas Selections:
- Christmas Bells....................Tennyson 11
- On the Morn of Christ's Nativity.............Milton 12
- The Blessed Story...............W. Chaterton Dix 13
- Christmas Bells....................Longfellow 14
- Why?...........................Eugene Field 15
- Christmas Bells......................Selected 16
- Christmas Bells......................Selected 17
- A Merry Christmas and a Glad New Year.
  ....George Cooper 18
- On Christmas Day..............George Washington 19
- The Prince of Peace........................Lowell 19
- His Birthday....................Lucy Larcom 20
- This Happy Day....................Phoebe Cary 21
- The Star of Bethlehem.......William Cullen Bryant 21
- Bethlehem......................Phillips Brooks 22
- Palestine..........................Whittier 23
- Under the Holly Bough..............Charles Mackey 23
- A Hymn to the Nativity..............Ben Johnson 24
- Love................................Schiller 24
- A Christmas Cross...............Willis Boyd Allen 25
- Recitation for the Little Folks..............Selected 25
- A Christmas Song..................J. G. Holland 26
- The King of Kings.................Dr. Isaac Watts 26
- Land O' Dreams.........From "Primary Education" 28
- The First Christmas....................Selected 28
- How I Wish I Knew!....................Selected 29
- Christmas Song..................Emilie Poulsson 30
- The Christ-Child..............Mrs. F. Spangenberg 32
- Mistletoe...............................A. M. F. 32
- Mistletoe....................Frances R. Arnold 33
- Under the Mistletoe....................Selected 34
- December..........................Longfellow 35
- Good News..........................Selected 36

(7)

Christmas Selections—Continued:

The Little Fir-Trees	Evaleen Steen	37
The Baby Fir	Susan Coolidge	38
"Quite Like a Stocking"	Thomas Bailey Aldrich	39
A Secret	Mrs. G. M. Howard	40
Bird's Christmas	Celia Thaxter	42
Christmas Eve	Mary Mapes Dodge	43
Holly	From "Nature in Verse"	43
Christmas at Sea	Robert Louis Stevenson	45
Christmas in the Olden Time	Sir Walter Scott	45
Kahawaii's Christmas	Letitia Mackay-Walker	47
In the Garden	Grace Duffield Goodwin	51
A Christmas Wish	Selected	52
A Christmas Wish		53
A Schemer	Edgar L. Warren	54
A Telephone Message	Selected	54
Little Barbara's Hymn	Selected	55
Christmas Treasures	Eugene Field	59
Jest 'Fore Christmas	Eugene Field	59
A Christmas Story	Charles H. Allen	61
Hang Up the Baby's Stocking	Selected	63
Two Little Stockings	Selected	64
Annie's and Willie's Prayer	Sophia E. Snow	66
No Santa Claus	Selected	72
Christmas Eve at the North Pole	Selected	74
The Christmas Dream	Eben E. Rexford	75
When Santa Claus Comes	Elizabeth Sill	76
Mrs. Santa Claus	Selected	77
Santa Claus and the Mouse	Emilie Poulsson	80
Who Fills the Stockings?	From "Wide Awake"	81
What the Mother Goose Children Want for Christmas	L. F. Armitage	82
Christmas Morning	From "St. Nicholas"	84
The Mahogany Tree	Thackeray	85
The Christmas Spies	From "Little Folks"	86
Baby's Belief	Charles H. Lugrin	87
The Doll's Christmas	From "Popular Educator"	87
Christmas Jingles	E. S. W.	88
A Christmas Jingle	Susie M. Best	89
What Willie Wants	Selected	90

CONTENTS.

Christmas Selections—Continued:
Christmas Song	Selected	90
Santa's Message	G. W. B.	91
Shoe or Stocking	Edith M. Thomas	92
Santa's Coming!	A. J. B.	92
Christmas Greeting	G. W. B.	93
What Christmas Brings	Selected	94
When I am Big	From "Primary School"	94
Little Two-Years	F. E. Fryatt	95
Brownie Song	Allie M. Felker	96
Some of the Lessons of Christmas Day	Charles H. Allen	98

New Year Selections:
The New Year	Selected	101
The New Year	Violet Fuller	102
Ring!	From "Primary Education"	103
January	H. H.	103
A New Year Song	Laura E. Richards	104
Dance of the Months	Selected	105
The Jolly Young King	Mary D. Brine	106
It's Coming	Selected	107
Ring Out, Wild Bells!	Tennyson	107

Miscellaneous:
The Seven Little Sisters	108
The Honolulu Children	115

Thanksgiving Selections:
First Thanksgiving Proclamation		141
Thanksgiving Day	Henry Ward Beecher	142
Thanksgiving	Selected	143
The First Thanksgiving	Selected	143
The First Thanksgiving Day	Margaret J. Preston	144
Thanksgiving	Will Carleton	146
Thanksgiving Day	Selected	147
November	Selected	148
The Festival Month	From "Youth's Companion"	149
Goodbye, Little Flowers!	Selected	149
November	William Cullen Bryant	150

Thanksgiving Selections—Continued:

Chrysanthemums	Selected	150
Down to Sleep	H. H.	151
November Party	Selected	152
We Thank Thee	Ralph Waldo Emerson	153
We Thank Thee	Margaret Sangster	154
Praise God	Selected	155
Thanksgiving	"Housekeeper"	156
Pilgrims	Lowell	157
A Thanksgiving Prayer	Selected	157
Thanksgiving Hymn	Selected	158
Thanksgiving	Howells	158
To Whom Shall We Give Thanks?	Anon.	161
Harvest Hymn	Whittier	161
The Pumpkin	Whittier	162
A Thanksgiving Treasure	Cora J. Alberger	164
Thanksgiving Joys	Selected	165
His Golden Corn	Selected	166
Thanksgiving Day	L. M. Childs	167
Grandma's Pumpkin Pies	Selected	167
Out for a Walk	L. F. Armitage	168
A Boy's Opinion	Emma C. Dowd	169
Thanksgiving Letter	Ed. Gazette	170
Recitation for the Little Folks	Selected	171
Which?	Selected	172
Thanksgiving	Selected	172
John White's Thanksgiving	Selected	173
That Things are No Worse, Sire!	Helen Hunt Jackson	175
The Puritan's Thanksgiving	Selected	176
Among the Apples	T. S. Collier	180
The Cat's Thanksgiving Soliloquy	L. F. Armitage	181
The Orphan Turkeys	Mrs. H. E. Jenkins	183
Little Nut People	Selected	184
The Little Pilgrim Maid	Selected	186
Elsie's Thanksgiving	Margaret E. Sangster	187
A Mother Goose Entertainment	Elizabeth Lloyd	189
Ten Little Indians		199

TOYON.

A Book of Holiday Recitations.

CHRISTMAS BELLS.

The time draws near the birth of Christ:
  The moon is hid; the night is still;
  The Christmas bells from hill to hill
Answer each other in the mist.

Four voices of four hamlets round,
  From far and near, on mead and moor,
  Swell out and fall as if a door
Were shut between me and the sound.

Each voice four changes on the wind,
  That now dilate, and now decrease,
  Peace and good will, good will and peace,
Peace and good will to all mankind.

This year I slept and woke with pain,
   I almost wished no more to wake,
   And that my hold on life would break
Before I heard those bells again.

But they my troubled spirit rule,
   For they controlled me when a boy;
   They bring me sorrow touched with joy,
The merry, merry bells of Yule.
                   —Tennyson.

ON THE MORNING OF CHRIST'S NATIVITY.
(Extracts from the Hymn.)

It was the winter wild,
While the Heaven-born child
All meanly wrapped in the rude manger lies;
Nature in awe to him
Had doffed her gaudy trim,
With her great Master to sympathize.

  *   *   *   *   *   *   *   *

But peaceful was the night
Wherein the Prince of Light
His reign of peace upon the earth began;
The winds with wonder whist
Smoothly the waters kissed,
Whispering new joys to the mild ocean,
Who now hath quite forgot to rave,
While birds of calm sit brooding on the charmèd wave.

  *   *   *   *   *   *   *   *

Ring out, ye crystal spheres,
Once bless our human ears
    (If ye have power to touch our senses so),
And let your silver chime
Move in melodious time
And let the base of Heaven's deep organ blow,
And with your nine-fold harmony
Make up full consort to the angelic symphony.
                            —Milton.

THE BLESSED STORY.

Like charms to lull the dying year,
The Christmas bells are pealing;
And hark! once more from yonder sky
The angel's song is stealing.
For eighteen hundred years and more
That strain of peace and glory
Has come to glad the heart of men,
To tell the blessed story.
                      —W. Chaterton Dix.

CHRISTMAS BELLS.

I heard the bells on Christmas day
Their old, familiar carols play—
    And, wild and sweet,
    The words repeat—
Of peace on earth, good will to men.

And thought how, as the day had come,
The belfries of all Christendom
    Had tolled along
    The unbroken song—
Of peace on earth, good will to men.

Then, from the black, accursèd mouth,
The cannon thundered in the South;
    And with the sound
    The carols drowned
Of peace on earth, good will to men—

And in despair I bowed my head;
There is no peace on earth, I said,
    For hate is strong
    And mocks the song
Of peace on earth, good will to men.

Then pealed the bells more loud and deep—
God is not dead—nor doth he sleep!
    The Wrong shall fail,
    The Right prevail—
With peace on earth, good will to men.
                  —Longfellow.

WHY?

Why do bells for Christmas ring?
Why do little children sing?
Once a lovely, shining star,
Seen by shepherds from afar,
Gently moved until its light
Made a manger-cradle bright.
There a darling Baby lay,
Pillowed soft upon the hay;
And its mother sang and smiled,
"This is Christ, the holy Child."
  Therefore, bells for Christmas ring,
  Therefore, little children, sing!
                  —Eugene Field.

CHRISTMAS BELLS.

Those Christmas bells as sweetly chime
    As on the day when first they rung
So merrily in the olden time,
    And far and wide their music flung,
        Shaking the tall, gray, ivied tower,
        With all their deep, melodious power,
        They still proclaim to every ear
        Old Christmas comes but once a year.

Then he came singing through the woods,
    And plucked the holly bright and green;
Pulled here and there the ivy buds;
    Was sometimes hidden, sometimes seen,
        Half-buried 'neath the mistletoe,
        His long beard hung with flakes of snow,
        And still he ever carolled clear,
        Old Christmas comes but once a year.

The bells which usher in the morn
    Have ever drawn my mind away
To Bethlehem, where Christ was born,
    And the low stable where He lay,
        In which the large-eyed oxen fed;
        To Mary, bowing low her head,
        And looking down with love sincere;
        For Christmas comes but once a year.

Upon a gayer, happier scene
  Never did holly berries peer,
Or ivy throw its trailing green
  On brighter forms than there are here;
    Nor Christmas in his old armchair
    Smile upon lips or brows more fair.
    Then let us sing amid our cheer,
    Old Christmas still comes once a year.
                    —Selected.

CHRISTMAS BELLS.

O bells! sweet bells! across the years
  Half-gay, half-sad, your chiming;
Old joys ye tell, old sorrows swell
  Throughout your tender rhyming.

O happy bells! through coming years,
  We hear, in your glad sending,
The message still of peace, good will—
  All jarring discords blending.
             —Selected.

A MERRY CHRISTMAS AND A GLAD NEW YEAR.

Oh, bells that chime your sweetest!
  Oh, world of glistening white!
Oh, breezes blithely bringing
  A message of delight!
From leafless hill and valley
  But one refrain I hear:
"A merry, merry Christmas
  And a glad New Year!"

From humble home and palace
  The kindly voice is breathed,
From forest arch and pillar,
  And meadows snowy wreathed,
An echo from the angels,
  A paean of good cheer:
Hark! "Merry, merry Christmas
  And a glad New Year!"

Oh, light of heavenly gladness
  That falls upon the earth!
Oh, rapture of thanksgiving
  That tells the Savior's birth!
The golden links of kindness
  Bring heart to heart more near,
With a "Merry, merry Christmas
  And a glad New Year!"
      —George Cooper, in "Golden Days."

ON CHRISTMAS DAY.

Assist me, Muse divine! to sing the morn
On which the Savior of mankind was born;
But, oh! what numbers to the theme can rise?
Unless kind angels aid me from the skies!
      —George Washington.

THE PRINCE OF PEACE.

"What means this glory round our feet,"
 The Magi mused, "more bright than morn?"
And voices chanted clear and sweet,
 "To-day the Prince of Peace is born."

"What means that star?" the shepherds said,
 "That brightens through the rocky glen?"
And angels, answering overhead,
 Sang, "Peace on earth, good will to men."

'Tis eighteen hundred years and more
 Since those sweet oracles were dumb;
We wait for Him, like them of yore;
 Alas, He seems so slow to come!

But it was said, in words of gold,
   No time or sorrow e'er shall dim,
That little children might be bold,
   In perfect trust to come to Him.

All round about our feet shall shine
   A light like that the wise men saw,
If we our loving wills incline
   To that sweet Life which is the Law.

So shall we learn to understand
   The simple faith of shepherds then,
And, clasping kindly hand in hand,
   Sing "Peace on earth, good will to men."

And they who do their souls no wrong,
   But keep at eve the faith of morn,
Shall daily hear the angels sing,
   "To-day the Prince of Peace is born!"
                      —Lowell.

HIS BIRTHDAY.

It is His birthday, His, the only one,
Who ever made life's meaning wholly plain;
Dawn is He to our night! No longer vain
And purposeless our onward struggling years.
The hope He bringeth overfloods our fears,
Now do we know the Father through the Son.
O Earth, O Heart, be glad on this glad morn!
God is with man! Life, life to us is born!
        —Lucy Larcom. ("Popular Educator.")

THIS HAPPY DAY.

This happy day, whose risen sun
   Shall set not through eternity,
This holy day, when Christ, the Lord,
   Took on Him our humanity.

For little children everywhere
   A joyous season still we make,
We bring our precious gifts to them,
   Even for the dear Child Jesus' sake.
      —Phoebe Cary. ("Popular Educator.")

THE STAR OF BETHLEHEM.

As shadows cast by cloud and sun
   Flit o'er the summer grass,
So, in Thy sight, Almighty One!
   Earth's generations pass.

And while the years, an endless host,
   Come pressing swiftly on,
The brightest names that earth can boast
   Just glisten, and are gone.

Yet doth the Star of Bethlehem shed
    A luster pure and sweet,
And still it looks, as sure it led,
    To the Messiah's feet.

And deeply at this later day
    Our hearts rejoice to see
How children, guided by its ray,
    Come to the Savior's knee.

O, Father, may that holy Star,
    Grow every year more bright,
And send its glorious beam afar,
    To fill the world with light.
        —William Cullen Bryant.

BETHLEHEM.

O little town of Bethlehem,
    How still we see thee lie!
Above the deep and dreamless sleep
    The silent hours go by.
Yet in thy dark street shineth
    The everlasting light,
The hopes and fears of all the years
    Are met in thee to-night.
        —Phillips Brooks. ("Popular Educator.")

PALESTINE.

Blest land of Judea! Thrice hallowed of song!
Where the holiest memories, pilgrim-like, throng;
In the shade of thy palms, by the shore of the sea,
On the hills of thy beauty, my heart is with thee.
With the eye of a spirit I look on that shore
Where pilgrim and prophet have lingered before;
With the glide of a spirit I traverse the sod
Made bright by the steps of the angels of God.
—Whittier. ("Popular Educator.")

UNDER THE HOLLY BOUGH.

Ye who have scorned each other,
Or injured friend or brother,
　In this fast-fading year;
Ye who, by word or deed,
Have made a kind heart bleed,
　Come gather here!

Let sinned against and sinning
Forget their strife's beginning,
　And join in friendship now;
Be links no longer broken,
Be sweet forgiveness spoken,
　Under the holly bough.
—Charles Mackey.

A HYMN TO THE NATIVITY.

I sing the birth was born to-night,
  The Author, both of life and light;
The angels so did sound it.
  And like the ravished shepherds said,
  Who saw the light and were afraid,
Yet searched, and true they found it.
  What comfort by him do we win,
  Who made himself the price of sin,
To make us heirs of glory!
  To see this Babe all innocence;
  A Martyr born in our defense;
Can Man forget the story?
—Ben Johnson.

LOVE.

Have love! Not love alone for one;
  But man as man thy brother call;
And scatter, like the circling sun,
  Thy charities on all.
—Schiller. ("Popular Educator.")

A CHRISTMAS CROSS.

No fir-tree in the forest dark,
  But humbly bears its cross;
No human heart in God's wide world
  But mourns its bitter loss.

Yet Christmas-tide can clothe the fir
    In splendors all unguessed,
And bring to every suffering heart
    Its joy, its peace, its rest.

God rest you, then, my gentle friend,
    And take your cross away,
Or clothe it with radiance new
    On this glad Christmas Day.
—Willis Boyd Allen, in "Youth's Companion."
(From "Popular Educator.")

RECITATION FOR THE LITTLE FOLKS.

Little songs, all full of joy, little lips can sing;
Little voices, soft and sweet, may their tribute bring;
Little verses can express what we wish to tell
Of a loving care that keeps little folks so well.

Kindly on us little ones beams a Father's smile;
Tender care and watchfulness guard us all the while;
For the pleasant things we have, clothing, shelter, food,
We would, in our happy songs, show our gratitude.
—Selected. (In "Primary Education.")

A CHRISTMAS SONG.

There's a song in the air!
There's a star in the sky!
There's a mother's deep prayer
And a baby's low cry!
And the star rains its fire, while the Beautiful sing,
For the manger of Bethlehem cradles a King.
In the light of that star
Lie the ages impearled!
And that song from afar
Has swept over the world.
Every hearth is aflame, and the Beautiful sing
In the homes of the nations that Jesus is King.
—J. G. Holland. (From "Popular Educator.")

THE KING OF KINGS.

"Shepherds, rejoice, lift up your eyes,
   And send your fears away.
News from the region of the skies!
   Salvation's born to-day.

"Jesus, the God whom angels fear,
   Comes down to dwell with you;
To-day He makes His entrance here,
   But not as monarchs do.

"No gold, nor purple swaddling-bands,
   Nor royal shining things;
A manger for His cradle stands,
   And holds the King of kings.

"Go, shepherds, where the Infant lies,
   And see His humble throne:
With tears of joy in all your eyes,
   Go, shepherd, kiss the Son!"

Thus Gabriel sang: and straight around
   The heavenly armies throng;
They tune their harps to lofty sound,
   And thus conclude the song:

"Glory to God that reigns above,
   Let peace surround the earth;
Mortals shall know their Maker's love,
   At their Redeemer's birth."

Lord, and shall angels have their songs,
   And men no tunes to raise?
O may we lose these useless tongues
   When they forget to praise!

Glory to God that reigns above,
   That pitied us forlorn!
We join to sing our Maker's love—
   For there's a Savior born.
              —Dr. Isaac Watts.

LAND O' DREAMS.

A snowy white ship on a deep, silent sea
Lies waiting each night just for you and for me;
The flag on its mast like a white poppy gleams,
As we float far away to the dim Land o' Dreams—
As we float far away to the dear Land o' Dreams.

A garden there lies with "Sweet Dreams" all ablow,
Each pure as a star, and as white as the snow.
On the night before Christmas—on that night alone—
You may gather and keep one white dream for your own.
You may gather and keep one white dream for your own.
—From "Primary Education."

THE FIRST CHRISTMAS.

Once there lay a little baby
   Sleeping in the fragrant hay,
And this lovely infant stranger
   Brought our first glad Christmas day.

Though that day was long ago,
   Every child throughout the earth
Loves to hear each year the story
   Of the gentle Christ-Child's birth.

Shepherds on the hillside, watching
  Over wandering flocks at night,
Heard a strange, sweet strain of music,
  Saw a clear and heavenly light.

And they seem to see the beauty
  Of the eastern star again!
And repeat the angel's chorus,
  "Peace on earth, good will to men."
      —Selected. (In "Primary Education.")

"Little children, can you tell,
Do you know the story well,
Every girl and every boy,
Why the angels sang for joy
On the Christmas morning?"
      —"Primary Education."

HOW I WISH I KNEW!

Little stars, that twinkle in the heavens blue,
I have often wondered if you ever knew
How there rose one like you, leading wise old men
From the East through Judah, down to Bethlehem?

Did you see the costly presents there they brought,
As the three wise men the heavenly Baby sought?
Did you see the worship tenderly they paid
To the stranger Baby in the manger laid?

Did you see the mothers pleading through their tears,
For the babes that Herod slew in after years?
Little stars, that twinkle in the heaven's blue,
All you saw of Jesus, how I wish I knew!
—Selected. (From "The Primary School.")

CHRISTMAS SONG.

While the stars of Christmas shine,
   Lighting the skies,
Let only loving looks
   Beam from your eyes.

While bells at Christmas sing,
   Joyous and clear,
Speak only happy words,
   All mirth and cheer.

Give only loving gifts,
   And in love to take;
Gladden the poor and sad
   For love's dear sake.
—Emilie Poulsson, in "St. Nicholas." (From "Primary Education.")

THE CHRIST-CHILD.

"Little Christ-Child,
 He was given on Christmas Day—
In His name, let
 Children give the best they may.

"Ring a merry season,
 Joyous Christmas bells.
What a tale of wonder
 Your sweet pealing tells,
For one little Child's sake
 All the world is glad."

"In a manger, lying low,
 Oh, so very long ago,
Shepherds, coming from afar,
 Following a moving star,
Found the Christ-Child, fair and sweet,
 And they kissed His little feet—
Found the Christ-Child, fair and sweet,
 And they kissed His little feet.

To that manger, rough and old,
 Wise men brought their gifts of gold,
And adored Him with glad voice,
 Saying, "He has come, rejoice!"
And white angels, wondrous fair,
 Watched about the Infant there,
And white angels, wondrous fair,
 Watched about the Infant there."

THE OLDEN STORY.

Do you know the olden story
Of the star that led the way,
When the wise men sought the Infant,
That in Bethlehem's manger lay?
In the east it shone so brightly,
Then o'er Judah's hillside steep,
Where the shepherds lay in slumber
By their flocks of quiet sheep.

Have you heard how angels voices
Sang the sweet and solemn strain?
Glory in the Highest! Glory!
Peace on earth, good will to men!
Every year the wondrous story
Thrills our spirits with delight,
And that star through all the ages
Makes the world's dark pathway bright.
—Mrs. F. Spangenberg. ("Primary Education.")

MISTLETOE.

Thou mystic plant, Druid-revered,
  Gay Christmas sprig, Saxon-endeared,
Thou welcome, cherished parasite,
  An honored place waits thee to-night!
—A. M. F.

MISTLETOE.

Mistletoe clung to an old oak-tree.
"Woo!" said the owl; "Te-woo! Te-wee!
Christmas has come; it is naught to me.

"Your life, my pretty one, is not secure.
Man will discover you; then be sure
Those that give pleasure must pain endure."

Each berry shook on the mistletoe,
Waxy and round and white as snow;
Then to the owl it spoke: "Oh, no!

"It would be cruel to take away
Freedom and life on Christmas Day;
Man would be willing to let me stay."

"Woo!" said the owl; "beware of fate!
Faith in man, I fear, is too great."
Off he fluttered to find his mate.

Into the darkness that very night
Radiant shone the Christmas light,
Showing the owl a lovely sight.

Under the mistletoe children gay
Frolicked and laughed and romped in play,
Kissed each other and ran away.

Then said the mistletoe: "Only I
Pleasure like this can give—and die.
Envy my happiness. Friends, good-by."
—Frances R. Arnold, in "Harper's Young People."

What's the meaning of the cedar,
Holly wreaths and mistletoe
That today are beautifying
Many places that we know?
—Selected.

UNDER THE MISTLETOE.

Grandma, in your frame on the wall,
  Beautiful maid of the long ago,
Stately and slender, and blonde and tall,
With the pinched-in waist and the foot so small,
  Prithee tell—for I fain would know—
What did you on that Christmas-tide
When great, great-grandpapa made you bride?

Handsome and courtly and debonair,
  With his powdered queue and his Roman nose,
As richly dark as his bride is fair,
He rests a hand on your straight-backed chair
  To whisper to you, I suppose—
To whisper again as in long ago
When he kissed you under the mistletoe.

Say, beautiful bride in the antique dress,
  Say, beautiful bride, in your bridal white,
Did you let him gaze on your loveliness
Till lifted eyes did your heart confess
  As you led the dance on your wedding-night?
Did he press your hand as he bent to say
Sweet words—as the lovers do to-day?

Ah! courtly groom of the vanished years,
  Beautiful bride of the days long fled,
Dust, but dust are your hopes and fears,
Cold your kisses and dried your tears;
  But I hang here over your head,
A sprig of such Christmas mistletoe
As you kissed beneath in the long ago.
—"Good Housekeeping."

DECEMBER.

. . . . . With snow-white hair,
I come the last of all. This crown of mine
Is the holly; in my hand I bear
The Thyrsus, tipped with fragrant cones of pine,
I celebrate the birth of the Divine.
. . . .
My songs are carols sung at every shrine,
Proclaiming, "Peace on earth, good will to men!"
—Longfellow.

GOOD NEWS.

I've heard a pleasant piece of news
For children that are good,
A million lovely Christmas trees
Are waiting in the wood,
With tapering stems
That seek the sky,
They grow both tall and straight,
And boughs adorned
With clustering cones
The fir-trees stand and wait.
Indeed, the green procession
Is already marching down
From the forests on the mountain
To the children in the town.
—Selected.

THE LITTLE FIR-TREES.

Hey! little evergreens sturdy and strong!
Summer and autumn-time hasten along.
Harvest the sunbeams then, bind them in sheaves,
Range them and change them to tufts of green leaves.
Delve in the mellow mould far, far below, and so,
Little evergreens, grow! grow little evergreens, grow!

Gather all uttermost beauty, because—
Hark, till I tell it now—how Santa Claus,
Out of the northern land over the seas,
Soon shall come seeking you, evergreen trees!
Seek you with reindeer, soon, over the snow, and so,
Little evergreens, grow! grow, little evergreens, grow!

What if the maple flare flaunting and red?
You shall bear waxen-white tapers instead.
What if now otherwise birds are beguiled?
You shall yet nestle the little Christ-Child.
Ah the strange splendor the fir-trees shall know, and so
Little evergreens, grow! grow, little evergreens, grow!
—Eveleen Stein, in "St. Nicholas." (Primary Educator.")

THE BABY FIR.

The Christmas day was coming, the Christmas eve drew near;
The fir-trees they were talking low, at midnight cold and clear.
And this is what the fir-tree said, all in the pale moonlight:
"Now which of us will chosen be to grace the holy night?"

The tall trees and the goodly trees raised each a lofty head,
In glad and secret confidence, though not a word they said.
But one, the baby of the band, could not restrain a sigh:
"You will all be approved," he said, "but oh, what chance
    have I?"

"I am so small, so very small, no one will mark or know
How thick and green my needles are, how true my branches
    grow;
Few toys or candles could I hold, but heart and will are free,
And in my heart of hearts I know I am a Christmas tree."

The Christmas angel hovered near; he caught the grieving word,
And, laughing low, he hurried forth, with love and pity stirred.
He sought and found St. Nicholas, the dear old Christmas
    saint,
And in his fatherly, kind ear rehearsed the fir-tree's plaint.

Saints are all-powerful, we know, so it befell that day
That, axe on shoulder, to the grove a woodman took his way.
One baby girl he had at home, and he went forth to find
A little tree, as small as she, just suited to his mind.

Oh, glad and proud the baby fir, amidst its brethren tall,
To be thus chosen and singled out, the first among them all?
He stretched his fragrant branches, his little heart beat fast—
He was a real Christmas tree, he had his wish at last.

One large and shining apple, with cheeks of gold,
Six tapers and a tiny doll were all that he could hold.
The baby laughed, the baby crowed, to see the tapers bright;
The forest baby felt the joy, and shared in the delight.

And when at last the tapers died, and when the baby slept,
The little fir, in silent night, a patient vigil kept.
Though scorched and brown its needles were, it had no heart to
    grieve;
"I have not lived in vain," he said; "Thank God for Christmas
    Eve!"

    —Susan Coolidge, in "Primary Education."

"QUITE LIKE A STOCKING."

Just as the moon was fading
Amid her misty rings,
And every stocking was stuffed
With childhood's precious things,
Old Kris Kringle looked around
And saw, on an elm-tree bough,
High hung an oriole's nest,
Lonely and empty now.

"Quite a stocking," he laughed,
"Hung up there on a tree!
I didn't suppose the birds
Expected a present from me!"
Then old Kris Kringle, who loves
A joke as well as the best,
Dropped a handful of snow-flakes
Into the oriole's empty nest.
—Thomas Bailey Aldrich, in "Primary Educator."

A SECRET.

A tall fir whispered in the wood:
"I'd tell a secret, if I could."
Then all the dry leaves on the ground
Whisked up and down, and all around,
To see if they the news might hear,
And spread it quickly far and near.

But the tall tree answered not the call;
It bowed politely, that was all,
And flung its tassels to the breeze,
And looked the wisest of all trees,
But when I came beneath the tree
It whispered, "Yes, I'll tell it thee."

Then as I rushed in eager haste,
And threw my arms about its waist,
I held my breath that I might hear:
"My child, I'm coming soon to be
Your very own dear Christmas tree."
—Mrs. G. M. Howard, in "Child Garden."
(From "Primary Education.")

BIRD'S CHRISTMAS.

In the far-off land of Norway,
Where the winter lingers late,
And long for the singing birds and flowers
The little children wait;

When at last the summer ripens
And the harvest is gathered in,
And food for the bleak, drear days to come
The toiling people win;

Through all the land the children
In the golden fields remain
Till their busy little hands have gleaned
A generous sheaf of grain.

All the stalks by the reapers forgotten
They glean to the very least,
To save till the cold December,
For the sparrows' Christmas feast.

And then through the frost-locked country
There happens a wonderful thing:
The sparrows flock north, south, east, and west,
For the children's offering.

Of a sudden, the day before Christmas,
The twittering crowds arrive,
And the bitter, winter air at once,
With their chirping is all alive.

They perch upon roof and gable,
On porch and fence and tree,
They flutter about the windows
And peer in curiously,

And meet the eyes of the children,
Who eagerly look out;
With cheeks that bloom like roses red,
And greet them with a welcoming shout.

On the joyous Christmas morning
In front of every door
A tall pole crowned with clustering grain
Is set the birds before.

And which are the happiest, truly
It would be hard to tell;
The sparrows who share in Christmas cheer,
Or the children who love them well!

TOYON.

How sweet that they should remember
With faith so full and sure,
That the children's bounty awaited them
The whole wide country o'er.

When this pretty story was told to me
By one who had helped to rear
The rustling grain for the merry birds
In Norway, many a year,

I thought that our little children
Would like to hear it, too,
It seems to me so beautiful,
So blessed a thing to do—

To make God's innocent creatures see
In every child a friend,
And on our faithful kindness
So fearlessly depend.
—Celia Thaxter.

CHRISTMAS EVE.

All night long the pine-trees wait,
Dark heads bowed in solemn state,
Wondering what may be the fate
Of little Norway spruce.

Little Norway spruce, who stood
Only lately in the wood.
Did they take him for his good—
They who bore him off?

Little Norway spruce so trim,
Lithe and free and strong of limb—
All the pines were proud of him;
Now his place is bare.

All the night the little tree
In the dark stood patiently,
Far away from forest free,
Laden for the morn.

Chained and laden, but intent
On the pines his thoughts were bent,
They might tell him what it meant,
If he could but go!

Morning came. The children,"See!"
Oh, our glorious Christmas tree!"
Gifts for every one had he;
Then he understood!
 —Mary Mapes Dodge. ("Primary School").

HOLLY.

Not one pretty flower would stay
When old Autumn nipped the grass;
For she had a cruel way,
Though as red-cheeked as a lass.
Winter had our Northland taken,
Her white flags by winds unshaken.

What, then, was there bright enough
  For the merry Christmas day?
"Good Dame Nature, be less rough,"
  Said the folks. "Leave storms, we pray;
Bring some posies and be cheery,
Lest she find the world too dreary."

"What are posies in the gleam
  Of my beautiful white frost?"
Said the old dame from her dream:
  "By the hedge, all snow-embossed,
Bloom itself the glad day carries,"
And she held up holly berries.

How their scarlet brightness shone
  In the morning's airy tracks!
Nature is a wise old crone—
  She knows what a picture lacks,
Winter lost its melancholy
Christmas laughed to see the holly.

Since that hour, now far away,
  When time's tired wing was light,
In the path of Christmas day
  Always shine the berries bright:
And, 'mid all its tender folly,
Gleams the blush of Christmas holly.

—"Nature in Verse."

CHRISTMAS AT SEA.

(A Fragment.)

Oh, well I saw the pleasant room, the pleasant faces there,
My mother's silver spectacles, my father's silver hair;
And well I saw the firelight, like a flight of homely elves,
Go dancing round the china plates that stand upon the shelves.

And well I knew the talk they had, the talk that was of me,
Of the shadows on the household, and the son that went to sea:
And, oh, the wicked fool I seemed, in every kind of way,
To be here and hauling frozen ropes on blessed Christmas Day.
—Robert Louis Stevenson.

CHRISTMAS IN THE OLDEN TIME.

(From "Marmion.")

On Christmas Eve the bells were rung,
On Christmas Eve the mass was sung—
That only night in all the year
Saw the stoled priest the chalice rear.
The damsel donned her kirtle sheen;
The hall was dressed in holly green;
Forth to the wood did merry men go
To gather in the mistletoe.
Then opened wide the baron's hall
To vassal, tenant, serf, and all.
Power laid his rod of rule aside,
And Ceremony doffed his pride.

The heir, with roses in his shoes,
That night might village partner choose;
The lord, underogating, share
The vulger game of "post and pair";
All hailed with uncontrolled delight
And general voice that happy night,
That to the cottage, as the crown,
Brought tidings of salvation down.
The fire, with well-dried logs supplied,
Went roaring up the chimney wide;
The table bore upon its board
No mark to part the squire and lord.
Then was brought in the lusty brawn
By old blue-coated serving-man;
The grim boar's head then frowned on high,
Crested with bay and rosemary.
There the huge sirloin reeked; hard by
Plum pudding stood, and Christmas pie;
Nor failed old Scotland to produce
At such high tide her savory goose.
Then came the merry masquers in
And carol roared with blithesome din.
England was merry England when
Old Christmas brought her sport again.
'Twas Christmas broached the mightest ale,
'Twas Christmas told the merriest tale;
A Christmas gambol oft would cheer
The poor man's heart through half the year.

—Sir Walter Scott.

"Within the hall are song and laughter,
  The cheeks of Christmas glow red and jolly,
And sprouting is every corbel and rafter
  With lightsome green of ivy and holly;
Through the deep gulf of the chimney wide
Wallows the Yule-log's roaring tide."
—"Popular Educator."

KAHAWAII'S CHRISTMAS.

Somewhere on a sheltered island
  Where the birds coo night and day,
And the palm-trees in their glory
  'Neath the gentle breezes sway,
Far away from snowy mountains,
  Somewhere on Oahu's shore,
Lived a wee Hawaiian maiden,
  Kahawaii's name she bore.

She had heard a strange, sweet story,
  One of old and lasting fame,
One that's loved alike by children
  Whatsoe'er their country's name.
She had heard the pale-faced stranger
  Who had come o'er ocean wide,
Tell the story of the Christ-Child
  And the happy Christmas-tide.

TOYON.

She had heard of dear old Santa,
   With his jolly, laughing face,
How he scrambles down the chimney,
   Pausing at the big fireplace;
She had heard he loved all children,
   Whether white or black or brown;
That he makes his yearly visits
   From the hovel to the crown.

Oft the little maiden pondered
   O'er the wondrous tales she heard.
She was puzzled why dear Santa
   To her home sent not a word.
Had he passed her humble dwelling,
   Knowing not a child was there,
Or, perhaps, had he forgotten
   That she lived on isle so fair?

It was drawing near to Christmas
   In the land across the sea,
When the holly-berries ripen,
   And all hearts are full of glee,
That the little brown wahine
   Sat beneath the cocoa palm,
Listening to the saucy mynah
   Piping through the evening's calm.

As she gazed across the water,
   Then into the starlit skies,
Soon her little lips did quiver,
   And a prayer was heard to rise:

"Moi Nui, I don't know you,
  But I'm sure you are somewhere;
Send kind Santa to our hale,
  Send a gift—this is my prayer.

"I have not a single plaything,
  Save the birds and bees and fish;
I've no brother and no sister,
  Send but one thing, if you wish.
Let me tell you, Moi Nui,
  When Santa leaves the land of storm,
He can cast his furs behind him,
  For he'll find it very warm.

"In Oahu there's no snowstorm,
  Even in December's night,
But you'll find the bright stars shining
  Or a rainbow's gorgeous light.
I shall thank you for your kindness
  When my present may appear,
And I'll be a good, kind daughter
  Every day throughout the year."

Christmas morn broke bright and cloudless,
  Early Kahawaii came
To the bedside of her mother
  For her morning kiss to claim.
In Makua's arms lay sleeping
  Dear old Santa's Christmas gift,
"Oh!" exclaimed wee Kahawaii,
  You're so tiny I can't lift."

Happy, happy Kahawaii!
  Underneath the cocoa palm
Warbling your own Christmas carol
  Sending forth a thankful psalm,
You have found just such a present
  As God gave that Christmas day
When the earth was waked from slumber
  By the heavenly choir's lay.
        —Letitia Mackay-Walker.

IN THE GARDEN.

There's a tender Eastern legend,
In a volume old and rare,
Of the Christ-Child in his garden
Walking with the children there.

And it tells this strange, sweet story——
True or false, ah, who shall say?
How a bird with broken pinion
Dead within the garden lay.

And the children, childish cruel,
Lifted it by shattered wing,
Shouting, "Make us merry music—
Sing, you lazy fellow, sing!"

But the Christ-Child bent above it,
Took it in his gentle hand,
Full of pity for the suffering;
He alone could understand.

Whispered to it—O so softly!
Laid his lips upon its throat,
And the song-life, swift returning,
Sounded out in one glad note.

Then away, on wings unwearied,
Joyously it sang and soared,
And the little children, kneeling,
Called the Christ-Child "Master-Lord."
—Grace Duffield Goodwin. ("Primary School.")

A CHRISTMAS WISH.

I'd like a stocking made for a giant
And a meeting-house full of toys,
Then I'd go out in a happy hunt
For poor little girls and boys;
Up the street and down the street,
And across and over the town,
I'd search and find them every one
Before the sun went down.

One would want a new jack-knife
Sharp enough to cut;
One would long for a doll with hair,
And eyes that open and shut;
One would ask for a china set,
With dishes all to her mind;
One would wish a Noah's ark,
With beasts of every kind.

Some would like a doll's cook-stove
And a little toy wash-tub;
Some would prefer a little drum
For a noisy rub-a-dub-dub.
Some would wish for a story-book,
And some for a set of blocks,
Some would be wild with happiness
Over a new tool-box.

And some would rather have little shoes
And other things warm to wear;
For many children are very poor,
And the winter is hard to bear.
I'd buy soft flannels for little frocks,
And a thousand stockings or so;
And the jolliest little coats and cloaks,
To keep out the frost and snow.

I'd load a wagon with caramels,
And candy of every kind,
And buy all the almonds and pecan nuts
And taffy that I could find.
And barrels and barrels of oranges
I'd scatter right in the way
So the children would find them the very first thing
When they woke on Christmas Day.

—Selected.

A CHRISTMAS WISH.

"If you could make a wish, my dear,
 And make but one," said I,
"Just one sweet wish for all the year,
 What should it be? Now, try!"

She thought a minute, gave a twirl,
 Her eyes began to shine;
"I'd wish that every little girl
 Could have a doll like mine!"

A SCHEMER.

Into a famous toy shop
Went little Joe and I
In the crisp Christmas weather,
To see what we could spy.

It was a place of wonder,
A real enchanted ground,
Where everything that heart could wish
Might certainly be found.

There were swings and rocking-horses
And sleds for boys and girls,
And games and books and puzzles
And dolls with flaxen curls.

Now find what she most wishes
(It popped into my head)
And get it for her Christmas,
And so I spoke and said:

"If you could have but one thing
Of all the things you see,
Now tell me, little daughter,
What that one thing should be."

The little maiden answered,
Scanning the treasures o'er:
"If I could take but one fing
I fink I'd take the store!"

—Edgar L. Warren.

A TELEPHONE MESSAGE.

"Ah! Here's the little round thing my papa talks into
To tell the folks down town what he wants to have them do.
I'm going to try, myself—now let me get a chair,
And then I'll stand on tiptoe so that I can reach up there.

Halloo! (that's what they all say)—you dear old Santa Claus,
I'm going to have a little bit of talk with you, because
I want to tell you all about a little girl I know
Who never had a Christmas in her life—she told me so.

I hardly could believe it, but she says 'tis really true.
I'm sure you're always very kind, but I'm surprised at you,
That you should have forgotten such a little one! but still,
You have, perhaps, all the stockings you can fill.

But, could you go to her house instead of coming here?
For mamma says that Christmas is the time of all the year
For children to remember poor litle girls and boys
Who never hang their stockings up for picture-books and toys.

And give her lots of goodies, too, because she's poor, you see,
And ought to have more sugar-plums than you could bring to me.
Now tell it on your fingers, and remember, as you go—
Just pack her little stocking to the very, very toe.

That's all—only, Santa Claus, I just would like to say,
If you should have more presents than you need on Christmas Day,
And could leave me just a few as you pass the chimney—why,
Of course—I would be very glad indeed. Good-bye! Good-bye!"

—Selected.

LITTLE BARBARA'S HYMN.

A mother stood by her spinning-wheel,
Winding the yarn on an ancient reel;
As she counted the threads in the twilight dim,
She murmured the words of a quaint old hymn:
"Whether we sleep or whether we wake,
We are His who gave His life for our sake."

Little Barbara, watching the spinning-wheel,
And keeping time with her toe and heel,
To the hum of the threads and her mother's song,
Sang in her own sweet voice ere long:
"Whether we sleep or whether we wake,
  We are His who gave His life for our sake."

Next morning, with bounding heart and feet,
Little Barbara walked the crowded street,
And up to her lips as she passed along,
Rose the tender words of her mother's song:
"Whether we wake or whether we sleep,
  We are His who gave His life for our sake."

A wanderer sat on a wayside stone,
Weary and sighing, sick and alone;
But he raised his head with a look of cheer,
As the gentle tones fell on his ear—
"Whether we wake or whether we sleep,
  We are His who gave His life for our sake."

A mourner sat by her loved one's bier,
The sun seemed darkened, the world was drear,
But her sobs were stilled and her cheeks grew dry,
As she listened to Barbara passing by—
"Whether we sleep or whether we wake,
  We are His who gave His life for our sake."

A sufferer lay on his bed of pain,
With burning brow and throbbing brain,

The notes of the child were heard once more,
As she chanted low at his open door—
"Whether we sleep or whether we wake,
We are His who gave His life for our sake."

Perhaps, when the labor of life is done,
And they lay down their burdens, one by one,
Forgetting forever those days of pain,
They will take up together the sweet refrain:
"Whether we sleep or whether we wake,
We are His who gave His life for our sake."
—Selected.

CHRISTMAS TREASURES.

I count my treasures o'er with care—
The little toy my darling knew,
A little sock of faded hue,
A little lock of golden hair.

Long years ago this holy time,
My little one—my all to me—
Sat robed in white upon my knee
And heard the merry Christmas chime.

"Tell me, my little golden head,
If Santa Claus should come to-night,
What shall he bring my baby bright—
What treasures for my boy?" I said.

TOYON.

And then he named this little toy,
While, in his round and mournful eyes,
There came a look of sweet surprise,
That spoke his quiet, trustful joy.

And as he lisped his evening prayer
He asked the boon with childish grace.
Then, toddling to the chimney-place,
He hung his little stocking there.

That night, while lengthening shadows crept,
I saw the white-winged angels come
With singing to our lowly home
And kiss my darling as he slept.

They must have heard his little prayer,
For in the morn, with rapturous face,
He toddled to the chimney-place
And found his little treasure there.

They came again one Christmas-tide—
That angel host, so fair and white!
And, singing all that glorious night,
They lured my darling from my side.

A little sock, a little toy,
A little lock of golden hair,
The Christmas music in the air,
A watching for my baby boy!

But if again that angel train
And golden head come back for me,
To bear me to eternity,
My watching will not be in vain.

—Eugene Field.

JEST 'FORE CHRISTMAS.

Father calls me William, sister calls me Will,
Mother calls me Willie, but the fellers call me Bill!
Mighty glad I ain't a girl—ruther be a boy,
Without them sashes, curls and things, that's worn by Fauntleroy!
Love to chank green apples an' go swimming in the lake—
Hate to take the castor-ile they give for belly-ache!
Most all the time, the whole year round, there ain't no flies on me,
But jest 'fore Christmas I'm as good as I kin be!

Got a yeller dog named Sport, sick him on the cat;
First thing she knows she don't know where she's at!
Got a clipper sled, an' when us kids goes out to slide,
'Long comes the grocery cart, and we all hook a ride!
But sometimes when the grocery man is worritted and cross,
He reaches at us with his whip, an' larrups up his hoss,
An' then I laff an' holler, "Oh, ye never teched me!"
But jest 'fore Christmas I'm as good as I kin be!

Gran'ma says that she hopes that when I get to be a man,
I'll be a missionarer like her oldest brother, Dan,
As was et up by the cannibuls that lives in Ceylon's Isle,
Where every prospeck pleases, an' only man is vile!
But Gran'ma she has never been to see a Wild West show,
Nor read the life of Daniel Boone or else I guess she'd know,
That Buffalo Bill an' cowboys is good enough for me!
Except jest 'fore Christmas, when I'm as good as I kin be!

And then old Sport he hangs around so solemn-like an' still,
His eyes they seem a-saying: "What's the matter, little Bill?"
The old cat sneaks down off her perch an' wonders what's become
Of them two enimies of hern that used to make things hum!
But I'm so perlite an' tend so earnestly to biz,
That mother says to father: "How improved our Willie is!"
But father, havin' been a boy hisself, suspicions me
When jest 'fore Christmas I'm as good as I kin be!

For Christmas with its lots and lots of candies, cakes and toys,
Was made, they say, for proper kids and not for naughty boys;
So wash yer face, and bresh your hair, an' mind yer p's and q's,
And don't bust out yer pantaloons, and don't wear out yer shoes;
Say "Yessum!" to the ladies, and "Yessur!" to the men,
An' when they's company, don't pass yer plate for pie again;
But, thinking of the things yer'd like to see upon that tree,
Jest 'fore Christmas be as good as yer kin be!

—Eugene Field.

A CHRISTMAS STORY.

'Twas a long time ago, say about eighteen twenty,
When matches were scarce and bellows were plenty,
In a neat little home, just outside of the city,
That there lived a young lass whom her people called Kittie.
She had pets for her comfort, and toys to amuse,
More of either, I think, than a young girl can use.

On the night before Christmas the clock had struck eight,
And Kittie was sleepy, but wanted to wait
Until mamma came home from a visit to town:
So, doffing her clothing and donning her gown,
She drew the big chair close up to the big fire,
The blaze from which mounted up higher and higher.
She waked up old Tabby, and, calling for Rover,
Sat down to think all of her Christmas hopes over.
She picked up the bellows that lay in the corner,
And sat up as happy as little Jack Horner.

Old Rover looked up, in his sad, quiet way,
As if wondering what his kind mistress would say.
While Tabby, afraid, but too jealous to hide,
Crept cautiously up on the opposite side,
Being ready, if all seemed just right, for the fun,
But if Rover looked cross, to spit, bristle and run.
Just look at a trio so happy and quiet—
Would you know how much comfort there is there, just try it.

"Now, Rover," says Kittie, "to-night's Christmas eve,
A time when good children expect to receive
Nice presents from Santa Claus, and for my share
I have hung up a stocking, see how it hangs there,
And mamma has gone to Santa Claus kind
To whisper what presents are most to my mind;
And for fear that my stocking would be much too small,
I have borrowed my grandma's to hang on the wall.

"Now big dogs and pussy cats don't care, you see,
For candy and dolls, and dishes for tea!
And if you did care, it could not be so,
For kittens and dogs don't wear stockings, you know;
And I guess," and she thoughtfully threw back her curls,
"There's a Santa Claus only for good boys and girls.
But then, in the morning, quite early, come here,
You shall each have a present, so never you fear;
Right under my stocking an elegant bone,
Which Rover may take and gnaw all alone;
And Tabby, whose coat is as flossy as silk,
Shall find there a saucer of elegant milk."

Now while Kittie was talking, her hearers to please,
She made each point clear by giving a squeeze
To the bellows, which puffed away into the blaze
In a way to make anyone start with amaze.
But tired and sleepy, at last she grew still
And her head dropped on one side, as sleepy heads will;
Old Rover lay down with his nose on his paws
As if patiently waiting for old Santa Claus.

And the cat softly purred, as she quietly crept
Into Kittie's warm lap, where she silently slept.
Here we bid them good night, with the hope that to-morrow
May bring "Merry Christmas," without care or sorrow.

—Chas. H. Allen.

HANG UP THE BABY'S STOCKING.

Hang up the baby's stocking,
Be sure you don't forget;
The dear little dimpled darling!
She ne'er saw Christmas yet;
But I've told her all about it,
And she opened her big blue eyes,
And I'm sure she understood it—
She looked so funny and wise.

Dear! what a tiny stocking!
It doesn't take much to hold
Such little pink toes as baby's
Away from the frost and the cold.
But then, for the baby's Christmas,
It never would do at all.
Why, Santa Claus wouldn't be looking
For anything half so small.

I know what we'll do for baby.
I've thought of the very best plan;
I'll borrow a stocking of grandma,
The longest that ever I can:

And you'll hang it by mine, dear mother,
Right here in the corner, so!
And write a letter to Santa,
And fasten it on to the toe.

Write, "This is the baby's stocking
That hangs in the corner here;
You never have seen her, Santa,
For she only came this year;
But she's just the blessedest baby!
And now, before you go,
Just cram her stocking with goodies,
From the top clean down to the toe."
—Selected. ("Primary School.")

TWO LITTLE STOCKINGS.

Two little stockings hung side by side,
Close to the fireplace, broad and wide.
"Two?" said Saint Nick, and down he came,
Loaded with toys and many a game.
"Ho! ho!" said he, with a laugh of fun,
"I'll have no cheating, my pretty one;
I know who dwells in this house, my dear;
There's only one little girl lives here."
So he crept up close to the chimney-place
And measured a sock with a sober face.
Just then a wee little note fell out
And fluttered low like a bird about.

"Aha! what's this?" said he in surprise,
  And he pushed his specs up close to his eyes,
  And read the address in a child's rough plan.
"Dear Saint Nicholas," so it began,
"The other stocking you see on the wall
  Is hung for a child named Clara Hall.
  She's a poor little girl, but very good,
  So I thought, perhaps, you kindly would
  Fill up her stocking, too, to-night,
  And help to make her Christmas bright.
  If you've not enough for both stockings there,
  Please put all in Clara's, I shall not care."
Saint Nicholas brushed a tear from his eye;
"God bless you, darling," he said with a sigh;
  Then softly he blew through the chimney high
  A note like a bird's when it soars on high,
  When down came two of the funniest mortals
  That ever were seen this side of earth's portals.
"Hurry up!" said Saint Nick, "and nicely prepare
  All a little girl wants where money is rare."
  Then, oh, what a scene there was in that room!
  Away went the elves, but down from the gloom
  Of the sooty chimney comes tumbling low
  A child's whole wardrobe, from head to toe.
  How Santa Claus laughed as he gathered them in,
  And fastened each one to the sock with a pin.
  When all the warm clothes were fastened on,
  And both of the socks were filled and done,
  Then Santa Claus tucked a toy here and there,
  And hurried away to the frosty air,

Saying, "God pity the poor, and bless the dear child
Who pities them, too, on this night so wild!"
The wind caught the words and bore them on high
Till they died away in the midnight sky;
While Saint Nicholas flew through the icy air,
Bringing "Peace and good will" with him everywhere.
     —Selected. ("Primary School.")

ANNIE'S AND WILLIE'S PRAYER.

(A Christmas Story.)

1.

'Twas the night before Christmas; "Good-night" had been said,
And Annie and Willie had crept into bed;
There were tears on their pillows and tears in their eyes,
And each little bosom was heavy with sighs,
For to-night their stern father's command had been given
That they must retire precisely at seven
Instead of eight; for they troubled him more
With questions unheard of than ever before.
He told them he thought this delusion a sin,
No such thing as "Santa Claus" ever had been.
And he hoped, after this, he should never more hear
How he scrambled down chimneys with presents each year,
And this is the reason why two little heads
So restlesly tossed on their soft, downy beds.

2.

Eight, nine, and the clock in the steeple tolled ten—
Not a word had been spoken by either till then;
When Willie's sad face from the blanket did peep,
And whispered, "Dear Annie, is you fast asleep?"
"Why, no, brother Willie," a sweet voice replies,
"I've tried in vain, but I can't shut my eyes;
For somehow it makes me so sorry because
Dear papa has said there is no 'Santa Claus;'
Now we know there is, and it can't be denied,
For he came every year before mamma died;
But then I've been thinking that she used to pray,
And God would hear everything mamma would say.
And perhaps she asked Him to send Santa Claus here,
With the sacks full of presents he brought every year."
"Well, why tan't we p'ay dest as mamma did then,
And ask Him to send him with presents aden?"
"I've been thinking so, too," and without a word more
Four bare little feet bounded out on the floor,
And four little knees the soft carpet pressed,
And two tiny hands were clasped close to each breast.

3.

"Now, Willie, you know we must firmly believe
That the presents we ask for we're sure to receive.
You must wait just as still till I say Amen!
And by that you will know that your turn has come then.
Dear Jesus, look down on my brother and me,
And grant us the favor we're asking of Thee;

I want a nice book full of pictures, a ring,
And a writing-desk, too, that shuts with a spring.
Bless papa, dear Jesus, and cause him to see
That Santa Claus loves as much even as he;
Don't let him get fretful and angry again
At dear brother Willie and Annie, amen!"
"Please, Desus, 'et Santa Claus tome down to-night,
And bring us some presents before it is 'ight.
I want he should give me a bright little box,
Full of ac'obats, some other nice blocks,
And a bag full of tandy, a book, and a toy,
Amen, and then, Desus, I'll be a dood boy."
Their prayers being ended, they raised up their heads,
And with hearts light and cheerful again sought their beds;
They were soon lost in slumber—both peaceful and deep,
And with fairies in dreamland were roaming in sleep.

4.

Eight, nine, and the little French clock had struck ten
Ere the father had thought of his children again;
He seems now to hear Annie's half-smothered sighs,
And to see the big tears standing in Willie's blue eyes.
"I was harsh with my darlings," he mentally said,
"And should not have sent them so early to bed.
But when I was troubled—my feelings found vent,
For bank-stock today has gone down ten per cent.
But of course they've forgot their troubles ere this,
And then I denied them the thrice asked-for kiss;
But just to make sure I'll steal up to their door,
For I never spoke harsh to my darlings before."

So saying, he softly ascended the stairs,
And arriving at the door heard both of their prayers.
His Annie's "bless papa" draws forth the big tears,
And Willie's grave promise fall sweet on his ears.
"Strange, strange, I've forgotten," said he, with a sigh,
"How I longed when a child to have Christmas draw nigh.
I'll atone for my harshness," he inwardly said,
"By answering their prayers, ere I sleep in my bed."

5.

Then he turned to the stairs and softly went down.
Threw off velvet slippers and silk dressing-gown.
Donned hat, coat and boots, and was out in the street—
A millionaire facing the cold winter sleet;
He first went to a wonderful "Santa Claus" store
(He knew it, for he'd passed it the day before),
And there he found crowds on the same errand as he,
Making purchase of presents, with glad hearts and free.
Nor stopped he until he had bought everything
From a box full of candy to a tiny gold ring.
Indeed, he kept adding so much to his store
That his various presents outnumbered a score!
Then homeward he turned with his holiday load,
And without Aunt Mary's aid in the nursery 'twas stowed.
Miss Dolly was seated beneath a pine tree
By the side of a table spread out for a tea.
A new writing-desk then near by it was laid,
And on it a ring for which Annie had prayed;
Four acrobats painted in yellow and red
Stood with a block-house on a beautiful sled;

There were balls, dogs and horses, books pleasing to see,
And birds of all colors were perched on the tree;
While Santa Claus, laughing, stood up in the top,
As if getting ready for more presents to drop.
And as the fond father the picture surveyed,
He thought for his trouble he had amply been paid;
And he said to himself as he brushed off a tear,
"I'm happier to-night than I have been for a year.
I've enjoyed more true pleasure than ever before.
What care I if bank-stock falls ten per cent more?
Hereafter I'll make it a rule, I believe,
To have Santa Claus visit us each Christmas eve."

6.

So thinking he gently extinguished the light,
And tripped downstairs to retire for the night.
As soon as the beams of the bright morning sun
Put the darkness to flight and the stars one by one,
Four little blue eyes out of sleep opened wide,
And at the same moment the presents espied.
Then out of their beds they sprang with a bound,
And the very gifts prayed for were all of them found;
They laughed and they cried in their innocent glee,
And shouted for papa to come quick and see
What presents old Santa had brought in the night
(Just the things they had wanted), and left before light.

7.

"And, now," said Annie, in a voice soft and low,
"You'll believe there's a Santa Claus, papa, I know."

When dear little Willie climbed up on his knee,
Determined no secret between them should be,
And told, in soft whispers, how Annie had said,
That their dear, blessed mamma, so long ago dead,
Used to kneel down and pray by the side of her chair,
And that God, up in Heaven, had answered her prayer!
"Then we dot down and prayed dust as well as we tould,
And Dod answered our prayers; now wasn't He dood?"
"I should say that He was, if He sent you all these,
And knew just what presents my children would please.
(Well, well, let him think so, the dear little elf,
'Twould be cruel to tell him I did it myself.)"

8.

Blind father! who caused your stern heart to relent?
And the hasty word spoken so soon to repent?
'Twas the Being who bade you steal softly upstairs,
And made you His agent to answer their prayers.
—Sophia E. Snow.

(This poem will suggest to parent or teacher a series of tableaux which may be presented while some child reads or recites the sweet old story.)

NO SANTA CLAUS?

(A recitation for an older pupil.)

Yes, there is a Santa Claus! He exists as certainly as love and generosity and devotion exist, and you know that they abound and give to your life its highest beauty and joy. Alas!

how dreary would be the world if there were no Santa Claus! There would be no childlike faith then, no poetry, no romance, to make tolerable this existence. We should have no enjoyment except in sense and sight. The eternal light with which childhood fills the world would be extinguished.

No Santa Claus! Thank God! he lives, and he lives forever. A thousand years from now—nay, ten times ten thousand years from now—he will continue to make glad the heart of childhood. —Selected.

A VISIT FROM SANTA CLAUS.

'Twas the night before Christmas, when, all through the house,
Not a creature was stirring, not even a mouse;
The stockings were hung by the chimney with care,
In hopes that Saint Nicholas soon would be there.
The children were nestled all snug in their beds,
While visions of sugar plums danced in their heads;
And mamma in kerchief, and I in my cap,
Had just settled our brains for a long winter's nap—
When out on the lawn there 'rose such a clatter,
I sprang from my bed to see what was the matter.
Away to the window I flew like a flash,
Tore open the shutters and threw up the sash.
The moon, on the breast of the new-fallen snow,
Gave a luster of midday to objects below;
When, what to my wondering eyes should appear,
But miniature sleigh and eight tiny reindeer,
With a little old driver so lively and quick,
I knew in a moment it must be Saint Nick.

More rapid than eagles his coursers they came,
And he whistled and shouted, and called them by name,
'Now, Dasher! Now, Dancer! Now, Prancer, and Vixen!
On, Comet! on, Cupid! on Donder and Blitzen!
To the top of the porch—to the top of the wall!
Now, dash away, dash away, dash away, all!"
As dry leaves that before the wild hurricane fly,
When they meet with an obstacle mount to the sky,
So up to the housetop the coursers they flew,
With the sleighful of toys—and Saint Nicholas, too.
And then, in a twinkling, I heard on the roof
The prancing and pawing of each little hoof.
As I drew in my head and was turning around,
Down the chimney Saint Nicholas came with a bound.
He was dressed all in fur from his head to his foot,
And his clothes were all tarnished with ashes and soot;
A bundle of toys he had flung on his back,
And he looked like a peddler just opening his pack.
His eyes, how they twinkled! his dimples, how merry!
His cheeks were like roses; his nose like a cherry;
His droll little mouth was drawn like a bow,
And the beard on his chin was as white as the snow.
The stump of a pipe he held tight in his teeth,
And the smoke it encircled his head like a wreath.
He had a broad face and a little round belly,
That shook when he laughed like a bowlful of jelly.
He was chubby and plump—a right jolly old elf;
And I laughed when I saw him, in spite of myself.
A wink of his eye and a twist of his head
Soon gave me to know I had nothing to dread.

He spoke not a word, but went straight to his work,
And filled all the stockings, then turned with a jerk,
And, laying his finger aside of his nose,
And giving a nod, up the chimney he rose.
He sprang to his sleigh, to his team gave a whistle,
And away they all flew, like the down of a thistle;
But I heard him exclaim, ere he drove out of sight,
"Happy Chistmas to all, to all a good night!"
—Clement C. Moore.

CHRISTMAS EVE AT THE NORTH POLE.

'Twas the night before Christmas, and at the North Pale,
Not a creature was stirring, not even a mole.
The stockings were hung by each little bear,
In hopes dear Saint Nicholas soon would be there.
Ma Bruin in kerchief, Pa Bruin in cap,
Had curled themselves snugly to get a good nap—
When up on the icebergs arose such a clatter,
They scrambled up quickly to see what was the matter.
The aurora shone bright on the snow and the ice;
'Twas like day, don't you know? And then, in a trice,
Appeared Santa Claus, laughing and jolly of face,
On the top of a berg; but he soon slid to base,
On a queer little sledge drawn by eight barking seals,
Strung all over with bells, which rang silvery peals,
While Santa Claus shouted to each one by name,
"Come, Sloppy! up, Floppy! hi, Duke! and ho, Dame!
Now, Freezer! now, Sneezer! on, Frappé! and hey,
Heap full the stockings. Ta-ra-boom-de-ai!"

The peanuts and candies he took from his store,
Tin monkeys and rattles, and forty things more
He crammed in the stockings, which grew in such size
It made the two Bruins most burst with surprise.
Then he wrapped himself warm from his toes to his hat;
The seals dressed in sealskin—of course you know that—
Got into the sledge, set all the bells ringing,
And the last that was heard of him gayly was singing
A rollicking song as he drove out of sight:
'Merry Christmas to all! to all a goodnight!"
—Selected.

THE CHRISTMAS DREAM.

Last Christmas time there was a lad about as big as I
Who ate too much plum pudding, and likewise too much pie.
He went to bed, and oh, dear me! what awful dreams he had!
Because his stomach was so full and felt so very bad.

He thought a great big bird, as black as ever crow could be,
Sat on the headboard of his bed and watched him solemnly.
And when he groaned in awful pain, this bird no one e'er saw
Spread out two big and flapping wings, and uttered "Caw!
    Caw! Caw!"

He thought a giant came to him and walked about his bed,
And put his fingers to his nose, and wagged his frightful head.
Then o'er the footboard of the bed he bent down very near,
And, "Would you like some pie?" he said, and grinned from
    ear to ear.

The poor lad went to sleep again, and what do you suppose?
He thought some most enormous rats were nibbling at his toes.
He tried to scream; he tried to kick; but not a sound made he,
For this unlucky lad was sick with nightmare pains, you see.

He groaned, and woke. "Oh, dear!" said he, "if things weren't made to eat,
Why do they taste so awful good, so tempting, and so sweet?"
Again he slept. The giant danced, the rats fell at his toes.
As "Caw! Caw! Caw!" the big bird screamed, and grabbed him by the nose,

He screamed, and then his mother came. "Poor boy!" said she, "I thought
That you would eat a great deal more than any creature ought."
And then she gave the suffering lad such horrid stuff to take,
He groaned and wondered which was worse—the medicine or ache.

They gave him good advice next day. He took it like a pill,
And what he said the night before, the lad repeated still:
"Things hadn't ought to taste so nice; for if a thing is good,
A boy don't know just when to stop, and couldn't if he would."
—Eben E. Rexford.

WHEN SANTA CLAUS COMES.

A good time is coming—I wish it were here!
The very best time in the whole of the year;
I'm counting each day, on my fingers and thumbs,
The weeks that must pass before Santa Claus comes.

Good-bye, for a while, then to lessons and school;
We can laugh, talk, and sing, without "breaking the rule";
No troublesome spelling, nor writing, nor sums,
There's nothing but playtime when Santa Claus comes.

I suppose I shall have a new dolly, of course—
My last one was killed by a fall from a horse;
And for Harry and Jack, there'll be trumpets and drums,
To deafen us all with, when Santa Claus comes.

I'll hang up my stocking to hold what he brings;
I hope he will fill it with lots of nice things;
He must know how dearly I love sugar-plums;
I'd like a big boxful when Santa Claus comes.

Then when the first snowflakes begin to come down,
And the wind whistles sharp and the branches are brown,
I'll not mind the cold, though my fingers it numbs,
For it brings the time nearer when Santa Claus comes.
—Elizabeth Sill, in "The Primary School."

MRS. SANTA CLAUS.

I think it is quite time
I took a little part
In all these Christmas joys
So dear to children's hearts.

TOYON.

For Santa Claus' name
Is known the wide world round;
And every year, with hearty glee,
His praises' children sound.

But Mrs. Santa Claus —
Indeed, whoever heard of her?
I shouldn't be at all surprised
If Santa'd left you to infer

There wasn't any Mrs. Claus,
Who stayed at home and mended toys,
And stuffed his pack and filled his sleigh
That he might bring you Christmas joys.

For many a year I've stayed at home,
As I was told all good wives did.
I kept the house, I fed the deer,
I did whatever I was bid.

But time has changed; my hour has struck;
The Twentieth Century woman's here,
And I have quite made up my mind
That I will drive each second year.

For I would not ungenerous be,
Of work I take an equal share;
Of pleasure, too, I ask a half—
I'm sure that's not more than fair.

I'm ready now to do my part,
So look for me, dear friends, this year,
And give to me a welcome warm—
I bring you joy and Christmas cheer.
—"Northwestern Journal of Education."

SANTA CLAUS AND THE MOUSE.

One Christmas eve, when Santa Claus
  Came to a certain house,
To fill the children's stockings there
  He found a little mouse.

"A merry Christmas, little friend,"
  Said Santa, good and kind.
"The same to you, sir," said the mouse;
  "I thought you wouldn't mind

"If I should stay awake to-night
  And watch you for a while."
"You're very welcome, little mouse,"
  Said Santa, with a smile.

And then he filled the stockings up
  Before the mouse could wink—
From toe to top, from top to toe
  There wasn't left a chink.

"Now, they won't hold another thing,"
  Said Santa Claus, with pride.
A twinkle came in mouse's eyes,
  But humbly he replied:

"It's not polite to contradict—
    Your pardon I implore—
But in the fullest stocking there
    I could put one thing more."

"Oh, ho," laughed Santa, "silly mouse,
    Don't I know how to pack?
By filling stockings all these years,
    I should have learned the knack."

And then he took the stocking down
    From where it hung so high,
And said, "Now put in one thing more;
    I give you leave to try."

The mousie chuckled to himself,
    And then he softly stole
Right to the stocking's crowded toe
    And gnawed a little hole.

"Now, if you please, good Santa Claus,
    I've put in one thing more;
For you will own that little hole
    Was not in there before."

How Santa Claus did laugh and laugh!
    And then he gayly spoke:
"Well, you shall have a Christmas cheese
    For that nice little joke."

If you don't think this story true,
    Why, I can show to you
The very stocking with the hole
    The little mouse gnawed through.
        —Emilie Poulsson. ("Primary School.")

WHO FILLS THE STOCKINGS?

Look where the stockings hang in a row!
Least and greatest, how they show!
Let lispers and toddlers still believe
Lapland Kriss on a Christmas eve
Lowers himself through the chimney black,
Lades each sock from his well-filled sack,
Leaps on his sleigh—and his reindeers go
Lightly over the frozen snow!

"Likely story!" you cry, and you
Laugh with your lips, and your eyes of blue.
Look sharply now—and look again—
Lesson in primer was never more plain:
Long stocking, short stocking, all show the same,
Large letter L, which stands for a name.
Love left his monogram written here—
Love fills the stockings, O children dear!
—"Wide Awake."

From earthland,
From skyland,
From some very highland,
Some wondrously shyland,
Old Santa Claus comes.
—Selected.

WHAT THE MOTHER GOOSE CHILDREN WANT FOR CHRISTMAS.

(To be recited by thirteen children in costume.)

(1.)
    Little Boy Blue would like a new horn
    For his will not make a sound;
    It rusted when he lay so long
    Asleep upon the ground.

(2 and 3.)
    And Jack and Jill want a water-pail,
    For theirs has been used so long
    For carrying water down the hill,
    It isn't very strong.

(4.)
    The woman who lived in the wonderful shoe,
    With so many children about,
    Says a nice, new shoe would suit her well,
    For hers is wearing out.

(5.)
    There's Mary Quite Contrary—well,
    The things that she longs for most
    Are silver bells and cockle-shells,
    For some of hers are lost.

(6.)
>And Jack Horner wants a large, fresh pie,
>Well stocked with many a plum,
>And hopes to find one every time
>That he puts in his thumb.

(7.)
>Now, what does Little Miss Muffet want?
>Why, a bowl for curds and whey,
>As hers got cracked when the spider came,
>And frightened her away.

(8.)
>And Simple Simon a penny wants,
>To take with him to the fair,
>That he may with the pieman trade—
>He'd like to taste his ware.

(9.)
>There's Mother Hubbard, the kind, old soul,
>She would like a nice, big bone
>For that hungry, gifted dog of hers,
>Whom all would like to own.

(10.)
>Mr. Peter, Pumpkin Eater, wants
>A much larger pumpkin-shell,
>For since his wife has worn big sleeves,
>She does not fit in well.

(11.)
>Bo-Peep really needs a shepherd's crook,
>For, when she awoke from sleep,
>She forgot to take her crook along
>While searching for her sheep.

(12.)
>Dr. Foster, who to Gloucester went,
>In that heavy shower of rain,
>Would like a pair of rubber boots
>Before he goes again.

(13.)
>But the boy who used to steal the pigs—
>That's Tom, the Piper's Son—
>Does not deserve a Christmas gift—
>He'll surely not get one.
>
>—L. F. Armitage.

CHRISTMAS MORNING.

They put me in the great spare bed, and there they bade me sleep:
I must not stir; I must not wake; I must not even peep!
Right opposite that lonely bed, my Christmas stocking hung;
While near it, waiting for the morn, my Sunday clothes were flung.

I counted softly, to myself, to ten, and ten times ten,
And went through all the alphabet, and then began again;
I repeated that Fifth-Reader piece—a poem called "Repose,"
And tried a dozen other ways to fall into a doze—

When suddenly the room grew light. I heard a soft, strong bound,
'Twas Santa Claus, I felt quite sure, but dared not look around;
'Twas nice to know that he was there, and things were going rightly,
And so I took a little nap, and tried to smile politely.

"Ho! Merry Christmas!" cried a voice; I felt the bed a-rocking;
'Twas daylight — Brother Bob was up; and oh, that splendid stocking!

—"St. Nicholas."

THE MAHOGANY TREE.

Christmas is here.
Winds whistle shrill,
Icy and chill.
Little care we:
Little we fear,
Weather without,
Sheltered about
The Mahogany tree.

Sorrow, begone!
Life and its ills,
Duns and their bills,
Bid we to flee.
Come with the dawn,
Blue devil sprite;
Leave us to-night
Round the old tree.

—Thackeray.

THE CHRISTMAS SPIES.

The little birds see all you do;
They hear each word you say;
They sit and talk about it, too,
When you are out at play.

And then to Santa Claus they go,
And tell him everything,
So, when, on Christmas, he comes by,
He'll know just what to bring.
—"Little Folks."

BABY'S BELIEF.

I believe in my papa,
  Who loves me, oh, so dearly;
I believe in Santa Claus,
  Who comes to see me yearly;
I believe the birdies talk
  On the boughs together;
I believe the fairies dance
  O'er the fields of heather;
I believe my dolly knows
  Every word that's spoken;
I believe it hurts her, too,

When her nose is broken.
Oh! I believe in lots of things—
I can't tell all the rest—
But I believe in you, mamma,
First, and last, and best.
—Charles H. Lugrin, in "St. Nicholas."

THE DOLL'S CHRISTMAS.

You mustn't think I'll tend you,
  Dolly darling, for you see
To-day I've very much to do
  And am as busy as can be.
Company's coming to-morrow, dear,
  Uncles and aunts and all,
Coming to spend their Christmas Day,
  And I can't attend to you, doll.

To-night I'll hang up your stocking, dear,
  And 'twill be filled with things so fine.
You know you hang them once a year,
  And then its Christmas-time.
To-morrow you'll wear your very best dress,
  And behave your prettiest way,
Now, go to sleep, dear; when you wake
  You'll find its come Christmas Day.
—"Popular Educator."

CHRISTMAS JINGLES.

Willy Wally
Had a dolly,
Hung it on a tree.
Went away,
Wind did play,
Humpty, dumpty dee!

A boy went out
With laugh and shout,
One Christmas long gone by.
The reason he
Was filled with glee,
This story shall tell why.

Old Santa had
Brought to the lad
A striped jumping-jack,
Which climbed a stick
So nice and slick
And slowly slid down back.

—E. S. W.

"The wrong shall fail,
 The right prevail,
 With 'peace on earth, good will to men.'"

"Hang up the vine and holly,
 Sign the cross over the door,
 That joy coming in with Christmas
 May go from the place nevermore.

To-day the Christ-Child reigneth,
In might of love alone,
A crowned and sceptered monarch,
And every heart his throne."

"A merry Christmas morning
To each and every one!
The rose has kissed the dawning,
And the gold is in the sun."

"And may the Christmas splendor
A joyous greeting bear
Of love that's true and tender,
And faith that's sweet and fair!"
—"Popular Educator."

A CHRISTMAS JINGLE.

With a clink and a clack,
And a great big pack,
　Down thro' the chimney,
　Pretty nimbly,
Somebody comes on Christmas Eve.

If we are real nice,
And as still as mice;
　If we never peep,
　And are sound asleep,
He'll fill our stockings, I do believe.

And when we arise
Next day, our eyes
  Will grow big to see
  How perfectly
He knew what we all wished to receive.
    —Susie M. Best. ("Primary School.")

WHAT WILLIE WANTS.

Dear Santa Claus:
You brought a sled
  To me a year ago;
And when you come again, I hope
  You'll bring along some snow.
        —Selected.

CHRISTMAS SONG.

(Tune, "Lightly Row.")

Christmas bells, Christmas bells,
How the merry music swells;
Loud they ring, loud they ring,
Santa Claus a welcome bring.
See his sleigh, how packed with toys,
Dolls for girls and skates for boys;
Bells ring clear, bells ring clear,
Santa Claus is near.

HOLIDAY RECITATIONS.

Christmas tree, Christmas tree,
Ready now for you and me,
Full of toys, full of toys,
Gifts for girls and boys,
Something there for every one;
Homeward now, his work is done,
Hear him cry, hear him cry,
"Little folks, good-bye!"

—Selected.

SANTA'S MESSAGE.

Santa writes: "Dear little girl,
   Pray tell me what you wish,
And, sure as sure can be,
   I'll bring it in a dish.

"And, little man, for what you like
   Write to old Santa's place;
For ball or top, boat or bike
   Must come through Santa's grace.

"Then hang your stockings up, my dears,
   For Santa Claus to fill,
And ask for things you ought to have
   That will not make you ill.

"And as your wishes are fulfilled,
   Just render thanks and say,
Dear Santa Claus, we wish that you
   Could come to us each day!'"

—G. W. B.

SHOE OR STOCKING.

In Holland children set their shoes,
  This night, outside the door;
These wooden shoes Knecht Clobes sees,
  And fills them from his store.

And here we hang our stockings up
  On handy hook or nail;
And Santa Claus, when all is still,
  Will plump them without fail.

Speak out, you "Sobersides," speak out,
  And let us hear your views;
Between a stocking and a shoe,
  What do you see to choose?

One instant pauses Sobersides,
  A little sigh to fetch—
"Well, seems to me a stocking's best,
  For wooden shoes wont stretch."

—Edith M. Thomas.

SANTA'S COMING.

Jingle, jingle, Christmas bells!
What a tale your chiming tells!
Little children, joyous, free,
Stand around the Christmas tree.

Eyes are sparking, voices ring,
Sweetly, sweetly, hear them sing!
"Come, dear Santa, come this way,
Come and join us in our play!"

Santa comes with laugh and shout,
Scatters presents all about.
Hear him cry, "Oh, children dear,
Merry Christmas, glad New Year!"
—A. J. B.

CHRISTMAS GREETING.

The Christmas bells are ringing,
  Over land, from sea to sea;
Their joyous tones are pealing,
  "Welcome, welcome, glad and free!"

In Bethlehem's born a Saviour,
  'Tis the Christ, our Lord and King;
Ah, listen! hear yon shepherds,
  Their joyous praises sing.

Oh, Jesus, loving Saviour,
  Thy blessings with us be!
We do, as little children,
  In faith look up to Thee.

Then as these bells are pealing
  Their glad and joyous sound,
"May peace, good will on earth"
  Thro' all the world resound!
—G. W. B.

WHAT CHRISTMAS BRINGS.

Merry Christmas always brings
Such a crowd of pretty things.
Useful, too—now, let me see
What it brings for you and me!
Caps and hats and mittens warm,
Scarfs to keep out wind and storm,
Cars and tops and sleds and books,
Loving words and happy looks.
—Selected.

WHEN I AM BIG.

When I am big I mean to buy
A dozen platters of pumpkin pie,
A barrel of nuts, to have 'em handy,
And fifty pounds of sugar candy.

When I am big, I mean to wear
A long-tailed coat, and crop my hair;
I'll buy a paper, and read the news,
And sit up late whenever I choose.
—From "Primary School."

LITTLE TWO-YEARS.

Little Two-Years (coming New Year's)
Hung her stocking up with pride,
While the fire, snapping, roaring,
Blazed within the chimney wide;
Then across the carpet, slowly,
Stole with tread as soft as snow
Little Two-Years (coming New Year's)
Pit-a-pat and tip-a-toe.

Sought her downy bed of blankets
Heaped with pillows, soft and white,
Little Two-Years (coming New Year's)
Meant to watch the livelong night—
Watch the mystic, wondrous chimney,
Down whose flue, so dark and wide,
Laden with a store of treasure,
Good old Santa Claus would slide.

Peeping from the snowy pillows,
Little Two-Years tried to think,
The fire so hot—how can old Santa—
Here her eyes commenced to blink;
The clock struck eight, the clock struck nine,
The hours she ceased to number,
The fire burned low, the little maid
Was wrapped in peaceful slumber.

All in the morning, bright and early,
Little Two-Years leaped from bed,
Ran across the crimson carpet
With a quick, impatient tread.
Reached her stocking, now o'erflowing,
Pulled it down with noisy glee,
Shouting, laughing, calling gayly,
"See what Santa has brought to me!"
—F. E. Fryatt.

BROWNIE SONG.

(Air, "Where do all the daisies grow?")

Where do all the Brownies go?
    I know, I know!
To the land of frost and snow;
Back they quickly come, you know,
Round the world, oh, ho, oh, ho!
    That is where they go;
Round the world, oh, ho, oh, ho!
    That is where they go.

Where do all the Brownies hide?
    Outside, outside,
Of the towns and cities wide,
In the wildwood they abide.
'Mong the flowers the Brownies hide,
    That is where they hide.
'Mong the flowers the Brownies hide,
    That is where they hide.

What do all the Brownies do
    For you, for you?
Look about for work to do;
Help you all be good and true;
Watch the flowers and guard them, too—
    That is what they do;
Watch the flowers and guard them, too—
    That is what they do.

Where do all the Brownies work,
    Work, work, work, work?
Chinese, Negro, Russian, Turk—
Brownies all, and never shirk?
Santa's shop is where they work,
    That is where they work;
Santa's shop is where they work,
    That is where they work.

What do all the Brownies make,
    Make, make, make, make?
Greatest pains the Brownies take
For the little children's sake—
Christmas gifts the Brownies make,
    These are what they make;
Christmas gifts the Brownies make,
    These are what they make.
          —By Allie M. Felker.

(This Brownie song should be sung or recited by several boys in costume. At the close, Santa Claus steps in and places a miniature Christmas tree on the floor or a low stand. Each Brownie pins a gift on it. Santa Claus, carrying the tree, then marches out, followed by the Brownies.)

SOME OF THE LESSONS OF CHRISTMAS DAY.

(To be read or recited by an older pupil.)

Of all the holidays that occur during the year, Christmas is looked forward to by most persons with the greatest pleasure. It is a festival day, bringing joy and gladness to thousands of homes—a day when boys and girls, even if they have outgrown Santa Claus and the stocking by the fireplace, expect, and in most cases receive, presents from those who love them.

It is probably true that many children are so interested in what they hope to have for Christmas presents, and afterward in the presents themselves, that they forget what the day really is.

Let us see if we cannot come to a clearer understanding of the day and what it should mean to us. You all know what a birthday is—for you have one every year, and it is doubtless celebrated in some way every time it comes.

Your birthday, however, is usually celebrated only by your own family, although, if you have a birthday party, others may come and aid you in its celebration. But, at best, there will be few to engage in it.

Sometimes we celebrate the birthdays of great men. The twenty-second of February, Washington's Birthday, is celebrated by nearly our whole nation. This is because he was a very great man. The day is, in most states, made by law a public holiday.

The Fourth of July is another birthday, the birthday of our nation, and you all know how widely that is celebrated. Not only all through our own country, but even in foreign lands, whenever two or more Americans can get together, they celebrate what we call the "Glorious Fourth."

But Christmas Day is a birthday celebrated far more widely than either of these. All over the Christian world, beginning on Christmas Eve, the day is recognized as the day of days. In all of England, in the most of Europe, in parts of Asia and Africa, as well as in many islands of the sea, Christmas is observed in much the same manner as we observe it—an almost universal holiday.

And all this is in remembrance of the fact that nearly nineteen hundred years ago, as we reckon time, there was born in the city of Bethlehem, a little baby boy. Born, not amid pomp and splendor, not even with the ordinary comforts of life, but in a lowly manger, surrounded by the "beasts of the field"—for, when His parents came up to visit Bethlehem, "there was no room in the inn."

Is it not a strange thing indeed that so many millions of people, year after year, unite in honoring the birthday of this manger-cradled Babe? And yet, His birth is the real reason for our keeping Christmas Day.

It is not for me to tell you the story of the wonderful life of this baby boy. You have heard much about it, and you will, all your life, be hearing much more. You will learn that we get but two short glimpses of this life until the boy became a man: that when He became a man, He began to teach, "Speaking as never man spake"; that for three years He went about doing good and teaching people, and that He was then put to death on the Cross.

You know where to find this whole story simply told, and you should read it very often and very thoughtfully. As you grow older you will come to know that the full lesson of this life is "The Greatest Thing in the World." If, in addition to the simple story in the Gospels the older ones of you can read "The Prince of the House of David," and "Ben Hur," it will help you to understand why we keep Christmas.

Now let us think what is the very best way to celebrate the birthday of so beautiful and sacred a life.

On your own birthday you often receive presents from your relatives and friends. These gifts mean that your friends love you and are glad that you were born; and, as you grow older, you will learn to prize these gifts more and more for this meaning instead of for their money value.

You will read that on the very first Christmas Day, the wise men brought gifts to the little Babe in the manger—gold, and frankincense and myrrh—the best treasures they had. But, as you cannot do this, what should you do? Do not think too much of what you are to receive, but rather what can you do to make this a happy Christmas Day for others.

First, if you have any ill will toward any one, let this day blot it out, for its first lesson is, "On earth peace, good will toward men." Second, as you cannot give gifts to this once baby boy, remember those who are in want, the poor or afflicted, for one of the best lessons He ever taught us is this: "Inasmuch as ye have done it unto one of the least of My brethren, ye have done it unto Me!"

There are two facts that children, and sometimes older people, are slow to learn; and yet, you will, I hope, by and by learn that both are true. However much pleasure the presents you receive give you, in almost every case they give a far greater pleasure to the givers; and, if it happens, as it often does, that there is something fitting that you particularly want and that your parents are unable to get for you, their inability to give is the cause of more pain to them than the lack of the gift brings to you. It is often so much more blessed to give than to receive.

The other fact is this: Whenever you harbor ill will toward a person it gives you far more unhappiness than it does him. He may be sorry every time he thinks of it, but you will positively be unhappy every time you see him, or think of him. You perhaps remember, in more than one case, the happiness that came from a full reconciliation.

If you take these two lessons to heart, you will have learned very much that will enable you to have a "Merry Christmas."
—Chas. H. Allen.

THE NEW YEAR.

Little children, don't you hear
Some one knocking at the door?
Don't you know the glad New Year
Comes to you and me once more?
Comes with treasures ever new,
Spread out at our waiting feet;
High resolves and purpose new
Round our lives to music sweet.

Ours to choose the thorns or flowers,
If we but mind our duty;
Spend aright the priceless hours,
And life will glow with beauty.
Let us then the portals fling,
Heaping high the liberal cheer;
Let us laugh, and shout, and sing,
Welcome, welcome, glad New Year!
—Selected.

THE NEW YEAR.

Ring, bells, from every lofty height.
An infant fair is born tonight;
Ring far and wide, ring full and clear,
To welcome in the glad New Year.
"The king is dead; long live the king!"
They said of old, and so we sing.
The Old Year has gone to his repose,
There let him rest beneath the snows.

Behind us, with the year that's gone,
Lie countless sins that we have done.
With joy we cast all care away
And pass into another day.
New day, new life, whose noble deed
With all our sinful years succeed.
A life of action, great and strong,
To cancel all we've done of wrong.
Ring, joyful bells, our hearts beat high
With faith and hope. Beyond the sky
Perchance the angels stand and wait
To catch the sound at Heaven's gate!
And echoing each silver tone,
Sing songs of praise around the Throne.
Ring, happy bells, to us is given
Still longer to prepare for heaven.
—Violet Fuller.

RING!

Ring! Ring! Ring!
A welcome to the bright New Year!
Life, Hope, Joy,
On his radiant brow appear!
Hearts with love are thrilling,
Homes with bounty filling.
Ho! ye wardens of the bells,
Ring! Ring! Ring!
Ring for winter's bracing hours,
Ring for birth of spring and flowers,
Ring for summer's fruitful treasure,
Ring for autumn's boundless measure,
Ring for hands of generous giving,
Ring for vows of nobler living,
Ring for truths of tongue or pen,
Ring "Peace on earth, good will toward men."
Ring! Ring! Ring!
Ring, that this glad year may see
Earth's accomplished jubilee!
Ring! Ring! Ring!
—"A New Year's Chime," in "Primary Education."

JANUARY.

Always a night from old to new!
Night and the healing balm of sleep!
Each morn is New Year's morn come true,
Morn of a festival to keep.

Only a night from old to new;
　　Only a sleep from night to morn.
The new is but the old come true;
　　Each sunrise sees a new year born.
　　　　　　—H. H., in "Primary Education."

. A NEW YEAR SONG.

When the year is new, my dear,
　　When the year is new.
Let us make a promise here,
　　Little I and you.
Not to fall a-quarreling
Over every tiny thing,
But sing and smile, smile and sing,
　　All the glad year through.

As the year goes by, my dear,
　　As the year goes by,
Let us keep our sky swept clear,
　　Little you and I.
Sweep up every cloudy scowl,
Every little thunder-growl,
And live and laugh,
Laugh and live,
　　'Neath a cloudless sky.

When the year is old, my dear,
　　When the year is old,
Let us never doubt or fear
　　Though the days grow cold.

Loving thoughts are always warm;
Merry hearts know ne'er a storm;
Come ice and snow, so love's dear glow
    Turn all our gray to gold!
—Laura E. Richards, in "Youth's Companion." (From "Primary Education.")

DANCE OF THE MONTHS.

The New Year comes in with shout and laughter,
And see, twelve months are following after!
First, January, all in white,
And February, short and bright.
See breezy March go tearing round;
But tearful April makes no sound.
May brings a pole with flowers crowned,
And June strews roses on the ground.
A pop! A bang! July comes in;
Says August, "What a dreadful din!"
September brings her golden sheaves;
October waves her pretty leaves,
While pale November waits to see
December bring the Christmas tree.
They join their hands to make a ring,
And as they dance they merrily sing,
"Twelve months we are, you see us here,
We make the circle of the year.
We dance and sing, and children, hear,
We wish you all a glad New Year!"
        —Selected. (From "Primary Education.")

THE JOLLY YOUNG KING.

There's a jolly young fellow, so blithe and merry
Who goes by the name of "January."
      He keeps out of sight
      Till a certain night,
      When old Father December
      Lies low on his bier,
      And his crown, you remember,
      Awaits the New Year.

This little new king, as he steps to his throne,
Makes many a promise that he will atone
For the faults of the old year, or many or few,
And no doubt the gay fellow does mean to be true
      To each and to all.

And here's to the health of the merry new king!
To his true, loyal subjects new joys may he bring!
      May the months be so glad
      That no heart may be sad!
May peace and prosperity walk hand in hand,
And doubt and perplexity flee from the land.
      For "A Happy New Year!"
      Cries young January;
      "I'm coming! I'm here!
      Let all hearts be merry."
         —Mary D. Brine, in "Primary Education."

IT'S COMING.

It's coming, boys; it's almost here;
It's coming, girls—the grand New Year.
A year to be glad in, not to be bad in;
A year to live in, to gain and give in;
A year for trying, and not for sighing;
A year for striving and hearty thriving;
A bright new year, oh, hold it dear;
For God, who sendeth, He only lendeth.
—Selected.

RING OUT, WILD BELLS.

Ring out, wild bells, to the wild sky,
The flying cloud, the frosty light!
The year is dying in the night;
Ring out, wild bells, and let him die!

Ring out the old, ring in the new,
Ring, happy bells, across the snow!
The year is going—let him go;
Ring out the false, ring in the true.

Ring out false pride in place and blood,
The civic slander and the spite;
Ring in the love of truth and right;
Ring in the common love of good.

Ring out old shapes of foul disease;
Ring out the narrowing lust of gold;
Ring out the thousand wars of old;
Ring in the thousand years of peace.

Ring in the valiant man and free—
The larger heart, the kindlier hand;
Ring out the darkness of the land;
Ring in the Christ that is to be.

—Tennyson.

THE SEVEN LITTLE SISTERS.

(Selections arranged from Jane Andrew's "Seven Little Sisters," and Frye's Primary Geography.)

Costume of Little Brown Girl: Cotton waist; striped shawl draped for skirt; strings of beads and bracelets; straight black hair, parted in the middle.

Costume of Agoonack: White canton flannel cloak with pointed hood trimmed in white fur; moccasins and mittens made of white canton flannel.

Costume of Manenko: Bandanna handkerchief wound around the head, turban style; red shawl, flowered calico skirt; face, arms, hands and feet blackened.

Costume of Gemila: White turban; plain white loose gown fastened at the back; bare feet; face blackened with burnt umber.

Costume of Jeanette: Plain white dress, full skirt, elbow sleeves, black velvet girdle; white stockings, black shoes; hair parted and hanging in braids.

Costume of Pen-se: Dark-blue silesia suit (Chinese blouse and pantaloons); white stockings, Chinese slippers.

Costume of Louise: White waist, red skirt, black velvet girdle; white stockings, black shoes; string of blue beads around the neck; flaxen hair braided in two braids and wound round the head.

The Seven Little Sisters enter from a side room to the platform, arrange themselves in a semicircle, and recite:

(All:)
>We, the Seven Little Sisters,
>Gay and happy joyous band,
>Come to greet and to amuse you—
>Each will tell you of her land.

(The Little Brown Girl steps forward, holds up a large brown doll and recites:)

This is the little brown baby. I brought her from the island of Java, southeast of Asia. Java is a land of fruit and flowers. It is so beautiful that people often call it the "Pearl of the East." Would you like to visit the litle brown baby's home? It is a pretty hut made of bamboo.

I am the little brown baby's sister. I help my mother keep the hut very neat and tidy. I stuff pillows with soft, white down that grows on a tree near by, and I weave grasses into mats which we use for beds. Then I cover them with pretty cloth.

My people eat rice, cocoanuts, and bananas. We like to drink the milk of the cocoanut.

The little brown baby and I live near the equator, where the weather is very hot. Our people send coffee over to you. I think coffee is not good for boys and girls to drink. What do you (looks at children in audience) think about it?

(The little Brown Girl steps back to her place.)

(Agoonack:)

Do you know me? I am Agoonack, the little Eskimo sister. I come from a cold country. They say that Santa Claus lives in a country near mine. He is a jolly old fellow. Have you ever seen his reindeer?

I live in an Eskimo hut made of blocks of stone. It looks like a great brick oven. The door is a low opening close to the ground, and one must creep on hands and knees to enter. There is another smaller hole above the door; it is the window. It has no glass—only a thin covering of something my father took from the inside of a seal, and my mother stretched over the window-hole, to keep out the cold and to let in a little light.

At my home we have three months of darkness, three months of light, and six months of twilight. We often see streamers of the great Northern Lights. Would you like to live in a cold country where is seen the aurora borealis, and where the great white bear and reindeer live?

(Manenko:)

I am Manenko, the little black girl. I come all the way from Africa. I have never been to school, although I am more than seven years old. I don't know how to read. I never saw a book but once.

I'll tell you what I can do. I can paddle my own canoe—on the river. I can hoe corn, and I can find wild bees' honey in the woods. I like to gather the scarlet fruit and help my mother pound corn in the great wooden mortar.

I live in a little, round house with low doorways most like those of a dog's house. We have a round, pointed roof, made of long rushes that grow by the river and braided together firmly with strips of mimosa bark; fine, soft grass is spread all over this roof to keep out the rain.

Of course, I am a negro. Many of my people have been taken from their homes in Africa and sold as slaves. In your land there are millions of black people, but they are all free.

We negro children are very fond of music. We keep time well, and we often make sounds like birds and running brooks. We have many games, also, and we like to dance and play ball.

(Gemila:)

I am Gemila, the little desert girl. I sleep in a tent. We have no furniture like yours—nothing but mats and low cushions called divans.

My people eat bread and dates. We drink camel's milk, and, when we can get them, we eat ostrich eggs. One is enough for our whole family.

I should not be happy if I had to live in a house, eat from a table, and sleep in a bed like yours.

(Gemila then sings or recites the following:)

> "I am Gemila, I am Gemila.
> I am a little desert girl.
> The desert is my home,
> And there I love to roam,
> For I am a little desert girl."

(Jeanette:)

I am Jeanette, the little Swiss mountain maiden. There is a fine story, "William Tell," written about some people in my country.

Have you heard about the Alps? They are beautiful, snow-capped mountains. My home is up among them.

(Jeanette now sings some pretty Swiss song or recites the following:)

SWITZERLAND.

"On Alpine heights the love of God is shed;
  He paints the morning red,
  The flowerets white and blue,
  And feeds them with His dew.
On Alpine heights a loving Father dwells.

"Down Alpine heights the silvery streamlets flow;
  There the bold chamois go;
  On giddy crags they stand,
  And drink from his own hand.
On Alpine heights a loving Father dwells.

"On Alpine heights the herdman tends his herd;
  His shepherd is the Lord;
  For He who feeds the sheep
  Will safe his children keep."

—Selected.

(Pen-se:)

I am Pen-se. I live in a boat on the river. People say that I am not a lady because my feet are large, but I'd rather be able to walk than to be the little Chinese girl who lives in the high-walled garden of the great house on yonder hill. She has small feet, and has to lie on her silken bed most of the time. Do you not think it cruel to bind up her feet in that way?

(Louise:)

I am Louise, the child of the beautiful River Rhine. I live where grapevines grow and where solemn old castles stand. Our dear Fatherland is much like your own country.

It is the dear Christmas time in our home. Ten days ago a lovely Christmas present came to us. Can you guess what it was? A little baby brother.

This year we shall have our Christbaum, or Christmas tree, at the foot of mother's bed. Tiny candles will burn all over this tree like little stars, and glittering fruit will hang among the dark-green branches. There will be presents for us all. Fritz will have a sword and Gretchen will have a big doll. I expect to have a workbox, some books, and perhaps a wheel. There will be nuts and candy for everybody, but we shall not take these off until New Year's Eve. That is the time to disrobe the Christmas tree.

We think our baby brother the dearest Christmas present of all. Let me tell you in song of the first and best Christmas presents the world ever had.

(Louise sings "The Story of Christ" in "Song Stories for the Kindergarten," by Mildred J. and Patty S. Hill. Published by Clayton F. Summy, 174-176 Wabash Avenue, Chicago.)

(All:)
>We hope our visit's given pleasure,
>Parents, friends, assembled here.
>We wish you all full Christmas measure
>And a gladsome, bright New Year.

THE HONOLULU CHILDREN.

Costumes.

1. Leialoha Kahalewai, age 8: Blue waist, blue overalls, panama hat, crown encircled by flower wreath, or lei; bare feet; face, hands, and feet, dark brown.

2. Luka Kapena, age 8: Navy blue sailor suit, trimmed with white braid; white sailor or island hat encircled with a lei; hair combed straight back and hanging in one braid; bare hands and feet; complexion, dark brown.

3. Ululani Lemon, age 14: White negligé shirt, black tie, white pantaloons, white belt, white sailor or island hat, tan shoes.

4. Lydia Aholo, age 14: White dress, white sailor hat, white stockings and white canvas shoes, white island fan.

5. Ah Kee, age 14: White shirt, white pantaloons, leather belt, grey cap; bare feet; complexion, yellowish brown; long black braid, or queue.

6. Ah Laan, age 12: Regular Chinese costume or dress like Luka Kapena's; complexion, yellowish brown.

7. Mary Dias, age 10: Red dress reaching to shoe tops, plain waist and belt, small shawl folded diagonally and pinned in front; hair, straight, parted in middle and reaching to shoulders.

8. Antone Silva, age 12: Colored shirt, blue overalls, leather belt, brown straw hat, bare feet.

9. Mrs. Kiku Nakayama, age 15: Gray silk kimono, a long, loose garment folded in front from left to right; flowing sleeves; obi, or wide sash, folded like a knapsack at the back; gray, white or lavender silk neck-piece; hair coiled high at the back of the head, and fastened with a tortoise-shell pin, tortoise-shell comb in front; white socks, sandals made of straw and fastened with velvet straps; Japanese fan, umbrella.

10. Take Matsui, age 14: Flowered kimono, white socks, sandals, light umbrella; complexion, yellowish brown.

11. Ruth Shaw, age 12: Thin, white dress, island hat, white shoes, white belt, white silk gloves, white island fan.

12. Hiram Bingham, age 15: White suit, tie, panama hat, white belt, white canvas shoes.

THE HONOLULU CHILDREN.

The Honolulu children march in by twos from a side room to the platform, arrange themselves in a semicircle, and recite in concert:

> From Oahu, in the tropics,
> An island famed in song,
> We bring Hawaii's greeting,
> "Aloha," sweet and strong.

The children then step forward in turn and recite their parts:

(Leialoha Kahalewai:)

How do you do? I am a little Hawaiian boy, and my name is Leialoha Kahalewai.

I live in Honolulu. Your people call our city the "Paradise of the Pacific." We call it Hawaii Nei.

I have to go to school every day when I am well. If I don't the truant officer comes after me. My people are sometimes called Kanakas, but we like better to be called natives, or Hawaiians.

We boys have great fun swimming about in Honolulu harbor. We swim out to meet the steamers, and we often dive for nickels and dimes which people throw into the water. We carry these in our mouths. Sometimes our cheeks are puffed way out they are so full of money. When the tide is low, we often wade out to the coral reefs and break off pieces of coral.

Did you ever see a surf-boat? It is fun to ride in one back from the coral reefs when the tide is high.

Come to Honolulu and I will show you our ricefields and taro patches. We make poi out of the root of taro. We are very fond of poi and fish. Sometimes we grind up cocoanuts and mix them with poi. We call this Hawaiian pudding. We eat pineapples, bananas, mangoes and alligator pears.

There are many spiders and insects here, but there are no snakes. I never saw a live snake in my life. We make pets of the frogs, spiders, and lizards; we carry them around in cans, boxes or bottles, and we often play with them all day long.

In Honolulu there are few birds, but out in the hills and on the other islands there are a great many kinds. Some of them are very beautiful. I wish you could see our fishes. They are of every size, shape, and color.

We used to have kings and queens in this country, but in August, 1898, the Stars and Stripes became our flag.

The Hawaiians all like music. Have you heard our band? Before the islands belonged to the United States the last piece always played by the band was "Hawaii Ponoi." Now the band plays "The Star Spangled Banner" after this Hawaiian national air.

(Luka Kapena:)

Do you wish to know my name? It is Luka Kapena. My father and mother live a long way off on another island. I have not seen them since I was a little girl. I live at a school called Kawaiahao Seminary. My father and mother do not come to see me because it costs too much, and it makes them sick to ride in the boat. Every year they send money to pay my tuition.

Shall I tell you what I like to do the best? I like to string flowers, seeds, and shells. We call each string a lei. We make and sell leis to the white people.

The little Hawaiian girls play just the same games as the boys. We like ball, tops and marbles, and we can all swim and ride horseback.

We have great fun on steamer days. We like it best when the Australia sails. Then the band plays, and everybody goes to the steamer. I like to ride down in a hack. Sometimes the people who go away are just covered with leis.

The Hawaiian children sing many pretty songs. We like the words and music of "Steamer Day." Listen and I will sing it for you:

STEAMER DAY.

I will make a lei,
   For 'tis steamer day,
Flowers yellow, flowers blue,
   I will string for you.

Leaves of maile, too,
   I will weave for you,
Green and sweet the maile lei,
   I will weave for you.

Friends who go away,
 Crowned with flower lei,
Think of those they left behind,
 Stringing flowers gay.

(For music of "Steamer Day" see "Simple Songs for Little Singers," by Anna B. Tucker.)

(Ululani Lemon:)

People call me a hapa haole. That means "half-white." My mother is Hawaiian and my father is English. I go to the Kamehameha School. It is one of the best schools in Honolulu. It is like a little city out at Kamehameha. There are many buildings; they have a church, a museum, halls, workshops, a school for girls, two for boys and a number of pretty cottages. The boys and girls are all or in part, native Hawaiians.

You must have heard of West Point, the greatest military school in the United States. The cadet suit I have on is like those worn by the boys at West Point. It is my Kamehameha uniform. Do you like it? We boys are good soldiers. We have a banner and a brass band of our own, and we always march when there is a royal funeral or procession in town.

We marched at the funeral of Queen Dowager Kapiolani. She was the wife of Kalakaua, the last king of Hawaii.

The Queen lay in state at her home for several days. On Wednesday at midnight she was brought to the native church. Her tenants followed, wailing and bearing burning torches made of kukui nuts. The church was beautifully decorated with yellow and purple, the royal colors, and there were many floral pieces.

For two days and nights services were held in the church. The Hawaiian Quartette sang many fine selections, and some of the oldest natives chanted just as our forefathers did in Polynesia one hundred years ago.

Have you ever seen a kahili? You would say it looks like a large feather duster. Eight Hawaiians waved kahilis over the queen dowager's casket. Royal funerals are held on Sunday. The natives always come over from the other islands to attend them.

Have you ever seen the picture of a catafalque? Kapiolani was put in a catafalque, and this was drawn by four hundred Hawaiian men dressed in black and white, and wearing yellow capes of silk or cotton. The kahili bearers wore capes of yellow feathers. These are made of the feathers of the Oo bird, which is now almost extinct. These birds are black, and they have a tuft of yellow feathers under each wing. In the Bishop Museum at our school there are many mantles made of Oo feathers; one is eleven feet long and thirty inches wide. How many birds do you think were killed in order to make these capes?

The queen dowager's funeral procession was a large one. First came the foot platoon of policemen, then the mounted police and the Portuguese band. Our Kamehameha boys and girls came next, and after them the pupils of the other schools and colleges. They were followed by the Hawaiian band, soldiers, and native societies. Then came the royal retainers, the bearers of the queen's crown and jewels, her physicians, the Protestant and Catholic clergy, the English choir and clergy, the four hundred linesmen and the kahili bearers, catafalque, and pallbearers. The two princes, David Kawananakoa and Jonah Kalanianaole, King Kalakaua's sister's children, followed in the queen dowager's carriage, and after them came the carriage of the ex-queen Liliuokalani. After the natives came the carriages of President Dole, his cabinet officers, and the diplomatic and consular corps. The general public in hacks, carriages, and on foot completed this royal procession.

Minute-guns were fired and bells were tolled for the good Queen Dowager Kapiolani, and all the people in Honolulu felt sad as she was carried to her last resting-place in the royal cemetery.

(Lydia Aholo:)

I, too, am a hapa haole. I go to the Kamehameha Girls' School. Our uniform is a white dress and a white sailor hat. I have come to tell you about a native feast given one Christmas night in the country a short distance from Honolulu. The feast was held in a shed of thatched grass, decorated inside with ferns and flowers. Over one hundred people came, and the men, women, and children all wore leis.

The long, low table, shaped like three sides of a square, was covered with ferns and ti leaves, and the food was piled high upon it. There were no plates, knives nor forks.

Liliuokalani was queen then. She stood at the head of the table, and we stood all around. After she was seated we sat on the ground and rested our arms on the table. Four Hawaiian girls waved kahilis over the queen's head all the time she was eating.

I wonder if you ever saw a calabash. It is a bowl made out of native wood. Chinese and Japanese servants passed calabashes of water. The people all washed their hands and dried them on ti leaves.

Poi was then passed in calabashes. We dipped the first two fingers of our right hand in this, gave them a quick twist, and then put them in our mouths. This is the way we eat poi. What do you suppose is meant by one-fingered, two-fingered, and three-fingered poi? Thick poi is eaten with one finger, thinner with two, and very thin with three.

When the poi was eaten, the waiters served roast pig to every one. Each piece was done up in ti leaves. We untied the leaves and ate the roast pig. Chicken, duck, and turkey were served in the same way. Afterwards, raw fish, baked fish and fried fish, also done up in ti leaves; raw sea urchins in the shell, live shrimps, and great balls of seaweed were passed and eaten. Look in the dictionary and you will see a picture of a squid. We ate many squids. Hawaiians like food you would not care to see on your tables. How would you like to eat a piece of roast dog? This is one dish of which the old natives are very fond.

Of course we ate bananas, pine-apples, and other tropical fruits. I could not begin to tell you all we had to eat and drink, but it was a great feast. Another word for feast is luau. Some day if you come to Honolulu you may be invited to a luau. The Hawaiians enjoy such feasts just as much as you enjoy your Thanksgiving dinner.

(Note.—In the "Youth's Companion," July, 1899, there is an accurate description of how poi is made.)

(Ah Kee:)

I am Ah Kee. I was born in a little village in China. I was not named until I was a month old; then I was washed in water in which leaves of the whampe tree had been boiled, and in which two duck's eggs and some copper coins had been placed. A good woman shaved my head, and the two duck's eggs were gently rolled over it. You will think this a queer ceremony. We call it "the touching of the hair." I was then dressed in a red jacket and green trousers, and a new cap was put on my head. My father and mother now spread out food, and worshipped, first, the goddess; second, the great spirit; and third, our ancestors. I was then named and taken into the temples where our people worship the gods. A lantern on which was written, "Longevity, Riches, Honor," was then lighted, and all our friends and relatives went with us to our house to enjoy what is called the "full month's feast."

When I was six years old I went to the village school. The teacher wore large Chinese goggles and a blue silk robe. I had to learn by heart everything in a book called the Tri-Metrical Classic; afterward I learned all there was in another book called the Chinese Classics. The teacher used to whack me over the head when I did not know my lessons.

Our people worship many gods and goddesses. When I was a little boy my mother often took me into the temple of the Goddess of Mercury, and we sometimes went into the temple of Kwan-Ti, the god of war; but we were not taught, as you are in the Sunday-school, to love the Chirst-Child and to keep the Sabbath day holy.

I was very happy in China. I had good times on such holidays as the "feast of the lanterns." My father and mother were always kind to me. They were very poor, and I had to go away to see if I could not make a little money to help them. I was sorry to leave them and go off to the "fragrant sandal-wood hills." That is what our people call the Hawaiian Islands.

It is a long way from my native village to Hong Kong. We had to take a boat and go down the river. On the way we were attacked by pirates. Many people were killed, but my uncle and I escaped. At last we reached Hong Kong and we went on board a great steamer. I had never seen so large a boat before, and for many days I thought I was riding on the back of a real dragon.

At first I was very much afraid of the people (foreigners), or Fan-Qui devils, as I had been taught to call them; but they were kind to me and I sooned learned to like them.

When we reached Honolulu my uncle took me to Mills' Institute, a large school for Chinese boys. Have you heard of Mr. Damon? He is at the head of this school. He is a good man. He and his wife are both very kind to the Chinese people. Mrs. Damon's father and grandfather were missionaries in China. She lived there many years, and she speaks Chinese as well as we do. Mr. Damon also speaks our language.

In Mr. Damon's school we study reading, spelling, geography, arithmetic, book-keeping, etc., and besides all this we learn to do all kinds of work. We like Mr. Damon because he helps us find work. All the Chinese boys like to work and earn money. We study the Bible and are taught to love God and to keep his commandments.

Every year Mr. Damon gives the Chinese boys and girls and their fathers and mothers a picnic. It is great fun. We play all kinds of running and jumping games. We always have a nice luncheon. The things I like best are cake, melon, pineapple, and soda water. We enjoy the ride we have on the tramcars or in carriages to and from the picnic.

(Ah Laan:)

My name is Ah Laan. I was born in China. When I was little my father was sick a long time, and he had to sell our rice plantation to get money to live on. By and by my father died.

My mother wanted to buy the plantation back. She had no money, so she sold me to a man named Sin Fong. I did not know that I was sold until my master took me on board a great ship. Then I knew that I was a slave-girl. There were many slave-girls on that ship.

Sin Fong, my master, brought me to Honolulu and got me a place to work. I had to earn money for him. Mr. and Mrs. Lum Ming, the people I lived with, were not good to me. Every day they strapped Ah Ming, their boy, on my back and made me carry him about the streets. He was almost as large as I, and the straps made great ridges on my shoulders. Mrs. Lum Ming kept a big Chinese servant who was always kind to me, but the second year she married and went away. Then I had to do all the work. I was too little to do the washing, but Mrs. Lum Ming made me wash way into the night. She was very unkind to me, and I wasn't at all happy.

Mr. Lum Ming sometimes sent me on errands. One day while out, I told a kind gentleman how Mrs. Lum Ming treated me, and he told me to run away the next time. I tried to do all the work; but one night I could not finish. Mrs. Lum Ming said I was lazy. When she tried to punish me, I ran away and hid. They brought out a lantern and looked for me everywhere, but they could not find me.

You have heard about the Chinese boys' school. Well, I went there in the middle of the night and I stood by the great wall until morning. One of the teachers, a kind gentleman, found me and took me to a girls' school, where there are a great many Hawaiian children, several Japanese, and a few Chinese girls.

My master tried to get me back, but the court would not let him have me.

The gentleman who found me has kept me in this girls' Seminary three years. He pays my tuition and is very kind to me. I like the school. It is my home. I live there all the time. I have learned to read, write and speak English. We also learn to sew, cook, and do housework.

Little Chinese girls who live with their fathers and mothers are very happy. When a baby girl is born, they say she brings good luck and gold pieces into the home. Sometimes her mother calls her Gold Piece, and she thinks it a very pretty name. They called me Gold Piece when I was little.

By and by I shall go out to work and earn money. Do you think I can earn enough to take me back to China? I should like to see my mother. She had to sell me. Maybe if she hadn't we should both have starved.

(Mary Dias:)

I am Mary Dias, a Portuguese girl. I live with my mother in Honolulu. She takes in washing. Grandmother lives with us. She sews all day long.

When I am not at school I take care of the baby for my mother, or go on errands, and do all I can to help her. Sometimes she gives my brother and me a basket of figs, papaias, or alligator pears; we sell these from house to house, and bring the money home to my mother. We go after washing and we take the clean clothes back to the people. Grandmother often sends us out with sewing.

We live up near Punahou College. Sometimes we ride down town on the tramcars with my grandmother. We go with her into the stores, and she lets us carry some of the packages.

We are always glad when Sunday comes. Father is with us then. We all go to church early in the morning, and visit with our friends the rest of the day. Once in a while we go to the beach at Waikiki and then to Makee island to hear the band play.

Once a year we have a Portuguese picnic. Do you like to ride on the steamcars? This year three hundred of our people went out to Pearl Harbor. We had a fine time at this picnic. There were music and dancing and many good things to eat and drink. Oh, it was fun to ride on the cars, out past the taro patches and ricefields. We passed several beautiful lakes, and saw a number of Chinese and Japanese villages. In the distance we saw sugar plantations. A planation is like a little village. There are houses, shops, and a large sugar-mill. Hundreds of Chinese, Japanese, and Portuguese work on these plantations.

(Antone Silva:)

I am a Portuguese boy. I was born in Honolulu but I now live with my father and mother on the Ewa sugar plantation. How many sugar plantations do you think there are on the Hawaiian Islands? There are sixty, and every year we send you many thousands of tons of sugar.

Perhaps you have seen sugar-cane growing. I help my father plant, cultivate, and irrigate it. How long do you think we have to wait before the cane is ready to cut? We wait a whole year and a half. Then we cut it down, strip it in the fields, and put it on the cars which take it to the sugar-mills.

Would you like to know how sugar is made? Sometime, when you visit Honolulu, get on the cars and ride out to Ewa plantation, and someone will show you through the large sugar-mill and tell you all you wish to know about sugar-making.

I work most of the time. I have no time for play except when I am at school. My people all work. Do you know where Madeira and the Azores are? The Hawaiian government brought out people from those islands to work on the sugar and rice plantations. Over seven thousand Portuguese children have been born here, and there are more than fifteen thousand of our people on the islands.

Have you seen the Hawaiian flag? The Portuguese people have always liked "Old Glory" best, and we are glad the stars and stripes now float over Hawaii Nei.

(Mrs. Kiku Nakayama:)

I am a Japanese lady. You can tell that I am married by the way I wear my hair. Do you know how long it takes to dress it? Twice a week the hair-dresser comes to my house and spends a whole hour dressing my hair. She uses much camelia oil. The Japanese never curl their hair. When I was a little girl I wore straight bangs. My hair was done up in the back and made to look like a bow of ribbon. A little tortoise-shell pin was run through it. When I was a young lady it was rolled up in front, puffed in the back, and made into a beautiful roll at the top. This was tied with a silk cord, and a tassel hung on each side. I wore a tortoise-shell comb just in front of the roll or puff. But now I wear it in this way. Do you like it?

The kimono I have on is made of silk crape; most of the Japanese ladies in Honolulu wear kimonos.

I was born in Tokio. My mother died when I was a little baby, and my father brought me to the "Paradise of the Pacific." He died soon after we landed and a kind lady named Mrs. Southworth took me to her home. She treated me as kindly as if I had been her daughter. I went to the public school and I was graduated from the high school. A lady said to me the other day, "Mrs. Nakayama, you speak the purest English I have ever heard in Honolulu." It made me very happy to hear that, for I have always tried to speak correctly.

Mrs. Southworth sent me through a kindergarten training school, and then I taught for three years in a Japanese kindergarten. There are many Japanese children in Honolulu and about forty thousand of our people in the Hawaiian Islands.

I am not teaching now. Two years ago I married a Japanese gentleman who is a cashier in one of the banks of Honolulu. We have a lovely home at Waikiki. Will you not come to see us some time? We are always pleased to entertain American ladies and gentlemen. We are glad to see the children, too. They are always welcome.

My husband and I attend the Japanese Methodist Church. There is a Japanese Congregational Church here, also. I have been to Japan twice. The first time I felt the winter very much, as the houses are built differently from yours. They have sliding doors made of paper, and great thick wooden outside doors which are opened in the morning and kept open all day. The rooms open into each other, and one can look right through the house.

There are no stoves or fire-places; there are instead, square fire-boxes, or braziers, which hold a few red coals. These braziers are not large enough to warm the whole body at once, but just the tips of one's fingers and nose. The gas that comes from these coals is very disagreeable.

There is no furniture to speak of in a Japanese house. The people sit on floor-mats and eat their meals from trays placed in front of them. They eat rice and fish, but they have a great many other dishes.

The children in Japan are very fond of games. One is like battledore and shuttlecock. Do you know how to play that game? They have another like jackstones; they play this with little crape bags filled with beans.

In Japan the plum and cherry blossoms are very beautiful, also the azalia, wisteria, and many other flowers. The chrysanthemum is the national flower. The Japanese name for chrysanthemum is kiku. I was named for that flower. Nearly every house has a garden in which are little lakes crossed by tiny bridges. In these lakes there are many pretty gold-fish swimming about.

The Japanese have many picnics and flower festivals. The children always enjoy these, but they like their own festivals better. Every year, on the third of March, the girls have a dolls' festival. Do you know the meaning of the word "heirloom"? There are five or six dolls in each family; these are heirlooms. Once a year they are brought out and kept on exhibition in the home for a whole month. Three times a day the little girls of the family and their friends carry food and place it on trays in front of these dolls. Each doll stands for some one in the royal family; one stands for the emperor and one for the empress. The children do not play with these dolls; but they have dolls with which they can play every day.

The dolls' festival always closes with a feast. The children eat the food which they set before their dolls. At the end of the month, the dolls are put away in boxes and the children do not see them again for a whole year.

On the fifth of May, the boys have a carp festival which also closes with a feast. The boys all have carps from five to ten feet long. These are made of paper or crape. They are filled with air and tied to the top of a long bamboo pole, and the boys watch them go swimming about in the air. The Japanese say that the carp is a sign of progress, and they teach their boys to make it a symbol of their lives. They say, "Our boys must aim high and follow in the line of progress."

The third of November is Emperor Mutsuhito's birthday. This is always celebrated by a state ball much like your governor's balls, and by many boat and horse-races. On this day, the Japanese towns and cities are beautifully decorated with bunting and flags, and there are many pretty fireworks. There were many emperors before Mutsuhito; they are all related. Japan has had one hundred and twenty-two emperors. Emperor Mutsuhito is a very sensible man; he does not think himself so much above the people as other emperors did, but he often rides about in an open carriage and goes freely among them. There were emperors in Japan six hundred and sixty years before the Christ-Child came to us.

Foreigners can now travel all over Japan without passports. Would you not like to see that country? It is very interesting.

(Take Matsui:)

Can you tell my nationality by my clothes? My name is Take Matsui and I came from Tokio. I do not wear a kimono every day. I have put this on to show you what my people wear in Japan. Most of the boys in Honolulu wear white duck suits; they are cool and confortable.

I work for a lady named Mrs. Reed. She lives on King street. I wash dishes, clean the floors, porches, and windows and take care of the lawns. Sometimes I go on errands.

Where do you think I like to go best? I like to go to the market. It is near the water-front and it covers a whole block. It is one of the most interesting places in Honolulu. The market is an open one. It is roofed to keep out the sun and rain. There are green lawns around it; these are protected by a fence. The space under the roof is divided into eight squares, and there are sixteen stalls in each square. Paved sidewalks pass through the market. I like to walk there when the place is all lighted up by electricity.

The stalls look like little stores, and one can buy whatever one wishes to eat or drink. Most of the groceries, fish, meats, fruit, and vegetables are brought in on cars over the little railroad which runs from the wharf near the pilot house up through a gateway into the front of the market. The merchants are Chinese, Japanese, and Hawaiians.

The fishermen sometimes come in from the boats and steamers with great baskets of fish, crabs, and lobsters. These fishermen are queer auctioneers. It is fun to see them bid off their fish to the merchants. The Chinese and Japanese all speak Hawaiian and most of the talking is done in the native language.

Wouldn't you like to see the fish? There must be over a hundred different kinds in the market, and they are of every size, shape, and color. Have you heard of the lady in Honolulu who spends most of her time in making paintings of fish? She has done fifty in water-colors. No two are alike. Perhaps some day you will see these paintings on exhibition in San Francisco.

There is one stall in the market just filled with dried fish. Some of these are very tiny. The natives are fond of dried fish. They also like to buy the baked fish, salt fish, and balls of seaweed. The merchants tie in ti leaves what they sell to the Hawaiians. The white people have their purchases wrapped up in paper.

The people of Honolulu do most of their marketing in the morning. Sometimes I go to the market with Mrs. Reed. She does the buying and I carry the packages for her. Mrs. Reed is very kind to me. I have worked for her ever since I left the Japanese school.

(Ruth Shaw:)

There is a sweet old Bible story about Ruth. Have you heard it? Mother likes to read it, so she named me Ruth. I, too, belong to the Hawaiian Mission Children's Society, and I have lived in Honolulu all my life.

I go to the Punahou Preparatory. It is a private school for white pupils. When we leave the Preparatory we go to the high school. We used to pay tuition there, too, but now it is free. The high school is very select; the boys and girls are all gentlemanly and ladylike.

I like to drive about Honolulu. There are many lovely homes surrounded by large green lawns. You will see sparrows everywhere. Listen, and you will hear the mynah bird scolding you, or the coo-dove singing mournfully. We think our hibiscus hedges, flowering trees and royal palms are very beautiful.

We are proud of our churches, schools and hospitals. Have you ever seen a palace? We have one in Honolulu. It is made of brick and the outside is cemented over. There are several fine government buildings. A few of these are made of coral, but most of them are built of lava stone. Some of the sidewalks are made of coral. Our city is lighted by electricity, and many of the houses have telephones.

I like to ride up to the top of Punchbowl, an extinct volcano. Then I can look all over Honolulu. Father often takes us up Tantalus Mountain. We spent last Fourth of July there. It is a fine, long, shady drive. We brought back many ferns. There are one hundred and fifty different kinds of ferns on the Hawaiian Islands.

The most fun is to drive out on the Waikiki road; then we see the Chinese gardens, the ponds where fish are fattened for market, and hundreds of ducks swimming about.

Last week we drove to the Pali up through the beautiful Nuuanu valley. The Pali is on the windward side of the island. The road is four miles long; we enjoyed the drive. When we reached the top, we looked over a cliff down, down, one thousand feet. Father told us that Kamchameha the Great drove the Oahu chiefs over this cliff. There is a statute of Kamehameha the Great in front of the Government building.

(Hiram Bingham:)

I am a grandson of one of the old missionaries who came to Hawaii in 1820. Have you ever heard of the blue book? In it are the names of the children and grandchildren of the missionaries. There are many of us, but we are now widely separated. We have an organization popularly known as the "Cousin Society," but its real name is the Hawaiian Mission Children's Society. Every year we receive letters from absent members. Some come from the United States, some from Japan, others from South America and Europe, and many distant countries. These letters keep us in touch with the missionary work done all over the world.

I attend the high school. This year I spent my vacation at the Volcano House on Hawaii, the largest of the eight islands. Father invited one of my classmates to go with us. We expected to have a pleasant trip, but we did not dream what was going to happen.

We had been at the Volcano House but a few days when Mauna Loa became active. The sides of this great volcano opened and lava spurted forth. The fountain of fire rose to a height of from one to two hundred feet and then fell in a burning river half a mile wide and four or five miles long. Mauna Loa was in action all the time we were on Hawaii, and father took us boys over the lava beds within a few feet of the burning river. During the three weeks we were there we never grew tired of looking at the volcano throwing out its steady stream of lava. We imagined we saw turrets, domes, and minarets. One night father said, "Look, boys, and you will see Eiffel Tower." I never expect to see a more beautiful sight than Mauna Loa in action.

There are a great many volcanoes on the islands, and the soil is not at all like that in your country. It is light and loose, and red or brown in color. I wish I had time to tell you all about these volcanoes. There are many interesting legends, some of which are better than any fairy tales you ever read. Perhaps when they are put in book form you will wish to read them.

(Note.—A very effective ending to this play would be the singing of one or more stanzas of "Hawaii Ponoi," the Hawaiian national air, found in "Simple Songs for Little Singers," by Anna B. Tucker.)

Pronunciation of Hawaiian Words.

(w has the sound of v)

Aholo	Ä hō′lō
aloha	ä lō′hä
Ewa	E′wä
hale	hä′le
hapa haole	hä pä hao′(how) le
Hawaii	Hä waī′ī
Hawaii Nei	Hä waī′ī Nei
Hawaii Ponoi	Hä waī′ī Pō nō ī′
Kahawaii	Kä hä waī′ī
kahili	kä hī′lī
Kalakaua	Kä lä kau′(ow) ä
Kalanianaole	Kä lä′nī ä nä ō′le
Kamehameha	Kä me′hä me′hä
Kapiolani	Kä pī′ō lä′nī
Kawaiahao	Kä waī ä hao′(how)
Kawananakoa	Kä wä′nä nä kō′ä
kukui	ku ku′ī
Leialoha Kahalewai	Lei′ä lō hä Kä hä′le wai
lei	lei
luau	lu au′(ow)
Luka Kapena	Lu′kä Kä pen′ä
maile	maī′le
makua	mä ku′ä
Mauna Loa	Mau (ow)′nä Lō′ä
Moi Nui	Mō ī′ Nu′ī
Nuuanu	Nu′u ä nu
Oo	Ō ʊ
Punahou	Pu nä hōw
Pali	Pä′lī
ti	tī
Ululani	U lu lä′nī
wahine	wä hī′ne
Waikiki	Waī kī kī′

Thanksgiving Selections.

FIRST THANKSGIVING PROCLAMATION.

"As the business of the year is now drawing toward a conclusion, we are reminded, according to the laudable usage of the Province, to join together in a gratful acknowledgment of the manifold mercies of the Divine Providence conferred upon Us in the passing Year: Wherefore, I have thought to appoint, and I do, with the advice of his Majesty' Council, appoint Thursday, the Third Day of December next, to be a day of public Thanksgiving, that we may thereupon with one Heart and Voice return our most Humble Thanks to Almighty God for the gracious Dispensations of His Providence since the last religious Anniversary of this kind, and especially for—that He has been pleased to preserve and maintain our most gracious Sovereign, King George, in Health and Wealth, in Peace and Honor, and to extend the Blessings of his Government to the remotest part of his Dominions; that He hath been pleased to bless and preserve our gracious Queen Charlotte, their Royal Highnesses, the Prince of Wales, the Princess Dowager of Wales, and all the Royal family, and, by the frequent encrease of the Royal Issue, to assure us the Continuation of the Blessings which we derive from that illustrious House; that He hath been pleased to prosper the whole British Empire by the Preservation of Peace, the Increase of Trade, and the opening of new Sources of National Wealth; and now particularly that He hath been pleased to favor the people of this Province with healthy and kindly Seasons, and to bless the Labour of their Hands with a Sufficiency of the Produce of the Earth and of the Sea.

"And I do exhort all Ministers of the Gospel, with their several Congregations, within this Province, that they assemble on the said Day in a Solemn manner to return their most humble thanks to Almighty God for these and all other of His Mercies vouchsafed unto us, and to beseech Him, notwithstanding our Unworthiness, to continue His gracious Providence over us. And I command and enjoin all Magistrates and Civil Officers to see that the said Day be observed as a Day set apart for religious worship, and that no servile Labour be performed thereon.

"Given at the Council Chamber in Boston the Fourth Day of November, 1767, in the Eighth year of the Reign of our Sovereign Lord George the Third, by the Grace of God, of Great Britain, France, and Ireland, King, Defender of the Faith, &c.

"By His Excellency's Command,   FRA. BERNARD.
"God Save The King."   A. Oliver, Sec'ry.

THANKSGIVING DAY.

Thanksgiving day is the one national festival which turns on home life. It is not a day of ecclesiastical saints. It is not a national anniversary. It is not a day celebrating a religious event. It is a day of Nature. It is a day of thanksgiving for the year's history. And it must pivot on the household. It is the one great festival of our American life that pivots on the household. Like a true Jewish festival, it spreads a bounteous table; for the Jews knew how near to the stomach lay all the moral virtues.

A typical Thanksgiving dinner represents everything that has grown in all the summer fit to make glad the heart of man.

It is not a riotous feast. It is a table piled high, among the group of rollicking young and the sober joy of the old, with the treasures of the growing year, accepted with rejoicings and interchange of many festivities as a token of gratitude to Almighty God.

Remember God's bounty in the year. String the pearls of His favor. Hide the dark parts, except so far as they are breaking out in light! Give this one day to thanks, to joy, to gratitude!

—Henry Ward Beecher.

THANKSGIVING.

Thanksgiving is a day set apart by government for acknowledging the mercies and the bounties we have received from God.

While we are joyous in meeting around our well-filled tables, let us not think our day well-spent until we have given from our store to bring cheer to some less fortunate neighbor.

—Selected.

THE FIRST THANKSGIVING.

The first Thanksgiving in New England was kept by our Pilgrim Fathers. The early settlers were without food, and suffered many hardships. The last of the corn had been eaten, and they had only a few nuts to sustain life. In their need a day of fasting and prayer was appointed.

On that day a ship came into harbor, bringing food for the starving colonists. The day of fasting was changed to one of thanksgiving, the first one kept in America.

—Selected.

THE FIRST THANKSGIVING DAY.

"And now," said the governor, gazing abroad on the piled-up store
Of the sheaves that dotted the clearings and covered the meadows o'er,
" 'Tis meet that we render praises because of this yield of grain;
'Tis meet that the Lord of harvest be thanked for his sun and rain.

"And, therefore, I, William Bradford (by the grace of God today,
And the franchise of this good people), governor of Plymouth, say,
Through virtue of vested power, ye shall gather with one accord
And hold, in the month of November, Thanksgiving unto the Lord.

"He hath granted us peace and plenty, and the quiet we've sought so long;
He hath thwarted the wily savage, and kept him from wrack and wrong.
And unto our feast the sachem shall be bidden, that he may know
We worship his own Great Spirit, who maketh the harvest grow.

"So shoulder your matchlocks, masters; there is hunting of all degrees;
And fisherman, take your tackle and scour for spoils the seas;

And maidens and dames of Plymouth, your delicate crafts
    employ
To honor our first Thanksgiving, and make it a feast of joy!

"We fail of the fruits and dainties, we fail of the old home
    cheer;
Ah! these are the lightest losses, mayhap, that befall us here.
But see! in our open clearings, how golden the melons lie!
Enrich them with sweets and spices, and give us the pumpkin
    pie!"

So, bravely the preparations went on for the autumn feast:
The deer and the bear were slaughtered; wild game, from the
    greatest to least,
Was heaped in the colony cabins; brown home-brew served for
    wine;
And the plum and the grape of the forest for orange and peach
    pine.

At length came the day appointed; the snow had begun to fall,
But the clang of the meeting-house belfrey rang merrily over
    all,
And summoned the folk of Plymouth, who hastened, with glad
    accord,
To listen to Elder Brewster as he fervently thanked the Lord.

In his seat sat Governor Bradford; men, matrons, and maidens
    fair.
Miles Standish and all his soldiers, with corselet and sword,
    were there;

And sobbing and tears and gladness had each in its turn the sway,
For the grave of sweet Rose Standish o'ershadowed Thanksgiving Day.

And when Massoit, the sachem, sat down with his hundred braves,
And ate the very riches of gardens and woods and waves,
And looked on the granaried harvest, with a blow on his brawny chest,
He muttered: "The Good Spirit loves His white children best!"
—Margaret J. Preston. ("Popular Educator.")

THANKSGIVING.

It is coming—it is coming—be the weather dark or fair;
See the joy upon the faces—feel the blessings in the air.
Get the dining-chamber ready—let the kitchen stove be filled;
Into gold-dust pound the pumpkins—have the fatted turkey killed;
Tie the chickens in a bundle by their yellow, downy legs;
Hunt the barn, with hay upholstered, for the ivory-prisoned eggs;
'Tis the next of a procession thro' the centuries on its way;
Get a thorough welcome ready for the grand old day.
—Will Carleton.

THANKSGIVING DAY.

Leaves of purple, scarlet, gold,
Bring sweet memories of old;
Far away a farmhouse lies,
'Neath the blue of sunlit skies,
And the days have shorter grown,
All the autumn grain is mown;
Oh, the hearts, so bright and gay,
Kept with us Thanksgiving day.

'Round the hearth the laughter rang;
Oh, the jocund songs we sang!
Years have kept those records dear
Of our youth's Thanksgiving cheer.
Lo! the day is here once more,
Fraught with memories of yore;
Visions of the feast, the joy—
Time can never these destroy.

Once again we join the glee,
And the season's revelry!
On the board the turkey lies,
'Round it ranged the pumpkin pies.
Ah, the good old-fashioned cheer!
Ah, the songs so sweet and dear!
Where are now the comrades gay
Kept with us Thanksgiving day?

Thanks we give for friendship old,
For love's blessings manifold;
Thanks for all that Time has brought,
All the kindness it has wrought;
In our hearts, oh! still may we,
Looking o'er life's rough sea,
Keep and honor while we may
Thoughts of thee, Thanksgiving day!
—Selected.

NOVEMBER.

My sisters are September and October, bright and gay;
They're beautiful in richer charms, while I am brown and gray;
Yet all their glorious days cannot compare with one I bring;
This one, the loveliest of the fall, Thanksgiving day, I sing.
—Selected. (From "Primary Education.")

THE FESTIVAL MONTH.

November has come with its festival day,
  The sweetest home feast of the year,
When the little ones mingle in frolic and play,
  And share in the Thanksgiving cheer.

And let us remember that tale of the past,
  Of the Pilgrims who gathered their band,
And offered up thanks for the corn when at last
  It waved o'er the famishing land.

For hunger had wasted those strong, patient men,
  Who struggled and labored in pain,
And the blessing of plenty which gladdened them then
  Gave courage and hope once again.

And the fame of their bravery never decays,
  While year after year rolls away,
Since the morning that ushered in prayer and in praise,
  The birth of our Thanksgiving day.
  —"Youth's Companion." (In "Primary Education.")

GOOD-BYE, LITTLE FLOWERS!

Hark! through the pine boughs,
  Cold wails the blast!
Birds south are flying,
Summer is dying,
  Flower-time is past.

Cold are November skies,
  Sunless and drear.
Golden-rod, eyelids close;
Asters, tuck in your toes;
  Winter is here!

"Good-bye, little flowers!"
  The icy winds sing;
Snow, blanket them over;
Sleep well, little clover!
—Selected. (In "American Primary Teacher.")

NOVEMBER.

Where are the flowers, the fair young flowers, that lately sprang and stood
In brighter light and softer airs, a beauteous sisterhood?
Alas! they all are in their graves, the gentle race of flowers
Are lying in their lowly beds, with the fair and good of ours.
The rain is falling where they lie, but the cold November rain
Call not from out the gloomy earth the lovely ones again.

The windflower and the violet, they perished long ago,
And the brier-rose and the orchis died amid the summer glow.
But on the hills the golden-rod, and the aster in the wood,
And the yellow sunflower by the brook in autumn beauty stood,
Till fell the frost from the clear cold heaven, as falls the plague on men,
And the brightness of their smile was gone from upland, glade and glen.
—From "The Death of the Flowers," by Wm. Cullen Bryant. (In "Popular Educator.")

CHRYSANTHEMUMS.

With summer and sun behind you,
With winter and shade before,
You crowd in your regal splendor,
Through the autumn's closing door.

White as the snow that is coming,
　　Red as the rose that is gone,
Gold as the heart of the lilies,
　　Pink as the flush of the dawn.
Confident, winsome, stately,
　　You throng in the wane of the year,
Trooping, an army with banners,
　　When the leafless woods are sere.
　　　　　—Selected. (In "Primary Education.")

DOWN TO SLEEP.

November woods are bare and still;
November days are clear and bright;
　　Each noon burns up the morning chill;
The morning snow is gone by night.
Each day my steps grow slow, grow light,
　　As through the woods I reverent creep,
　　Watching all things lie "down to sleep."

I never knew before what beds,
Fragrant to smell and soft to touch,
　　The forest sifts and shapes and spreads;
I never knew before how much
Of human sound there is in such
　　Low tones as through the forest sweep,
　　When all things lie "down to sleep."

Each day I find new coverlids
Tucked in, and more sweet eyes shut tight;
Sometimes the viewless mother bids
Her ferns kneel down full in my sight;
I hear their chorus of "Good-night!"
And half I smile and half I weep,
While they all lie "down to sleep."

—H. H.

NOVEMBER PARTY.

November gave a party—
  The leaves, by hundreds, came—
The Chestnuts, Oaks, and Maples,
  And leaves of every name;
The sunshine spread a carpet,
  And everything was grand;
Miss Weather led the dancing,
  Professor Wind, the band.

The Chestnuts came in yellow,
  The Oaks in crimson dress;
The lovely Misses Maple
  In scarlet looked their best.
All balanced to their partners,
  And gaily fluttered by;
The sight was like a rainbow,
  New-fallen from the sky.

Then, in the rusty hollows,
   At hide-and-seek they played.
The party closed at sundown,
   And everybody stayed.
Professor Wind played louder,
   They flew along the ground,
And there the party ended,
   In "hands across, all round!"
      —From "Song Stories for Little People."

WE THANK THEE.

For flowers, that bloom about our feet,
For tender grass, so fresh and sweet,
For song of bird and hum of bee,
For all things fair we hear or see—
Father in Heaven, we thank Thee!

For blue of stream and blue of sky,
For pleasant shade of branches high,
For fragrant air and cooling breeze,
For beauty of the blooming trees—
Father in Heaven, we thank Thee!

For mother-love and father-care,
For brothers strong and sisters fair,
For love at home and school each day,
For guidance lest we go astray—
Father in Heaven, we thank Thee!

For Thy dear everlasting arms,
That bear us o'er all ills and harms;
For blessed words of long ago
That help us now Thy will to know—
Father in Heaven, we thank Thee!
—Ralph Waldo Emerson.

WE THANK THEE.

For peace and for plenty, for freedom, for rest,
For joy in the land from the east to the west,
For the dear, starry flag, with its red, white and blue,
We thank Thee from hearts that are honest and true.

For waking and sleeping, for blessings to be,
We children would offer our praises to Thee;
For God is our Father, and bends from above
To keep the world round in the smile of his love.
—Margaret Sangster.

But O! Thou bounteous Giver of all good,
Thou art, of all Thy gifts, Thyself the crown!
Give what thou canst; without Thee we are poor,
And with Thee rich; take what Thou wilt away.
—Cowper.

PRAISE GOD.

(For Seven Pupils.)

(First:)
Praise God for wheat, so white and sweet, of which to make our bread.

(Second:)
Praise God for yellow corn, with which His waiting world is fed.

(Third:)
Praise God for fish, and flesh, and fowl, He gave to men for food.

(Fourth:)
Praise God for every creature which He made and called it good.

(Fifth:)
Praise God for winter's store of ice, praise God for summer's heat.

(Sixth:)
Praise God for the fruit-tree bearing seed, "to you it is for meat."

(Seventh:)
Praise God for all the bounty by which the world is fed.

(All:)
Praise God, ye children all to whom he gives your daily bread.

—Selected.

THANKSGIVING.

Oh, give thanks for summer and winter,
Give thanks for the sunshine and rain;
For the flowers, the fruits, and the grasses,
And the bountiful harvest of grain;
For the winds that sweep over our prairies;
Distributing vigor and health—
Oh, give thanks to our Heavenly Father
For nature's abundance of wealth!

Oh, give thanks for loved friends and relations,
For sweet converse with those that are dear;
Give thanks for our country's salvation,
From famine and war the past year;
That, while kingdoms and empires have fallen,
Our government firmly has stood—
Oh, give thanks to our Heavenly Father
For all this abundance of good!

Give thanks for each lawful ambition,
That gives a new impulse to do;
Give thanks for each fond hope's fruition,
And all of God's goodness to you.
Forget not whence cometh the power,
That all of these blessings secures—
Oh, give thanks to our Heavenly Father,
Whose mercy forever endures.

—Housekeeper.

PILGRIMS.

They must upward still and onward, who would keep abreast
    of Truth,
Lo, before us gleam her camp-fires! We ourselves must pil-
    grims be,
Launch our Mayflower, and steer boldly through the desperate
    winter sea,
Nor attempt the Future's portal with the Past's blood-rusted
    key.

—Lowell.

A THANKSGIVING PRAYER.

Oh, Thou, Grand Builder of the Universe!
Who mak'st the rolling worlds and peoplest them
With creatures—Who watchest the sparrow's fall
And shap'st the fate of nations—
Hear us, we beseech Thee! Bend low Thine ear,
And in Thy mercy heed, while now the Nation
Kneels with her thank-offering.
                        Another year
Upon the circled track of Time has passed,
And still she holds Thy favor. Oh! give her,
We implore Thee, a sense of all Thy blessings—
A full sense to know, so in the knowledge
She may worthier be to wear them.
        All this, O Great Supreme!
She lowly asks through him Thou lovest.

—Selected.

THANKSGIVING HYMN

To the Giver of all blessings,
  Let our voices rise in praise,
For the joys and countless mercies
  He hath sent to crown our days;
For the homes of peace and plenty,
  And a land so fair and wide,
For the labor of the noonday,
  And the rest of eventide;

For the wealth of golden harvests,
  For the sunlight and the rain,
For the grandeur of the ocean,
  For the mountain and the plain;
For the ever-changing seasons
  And the comforts which they bring,
For Thy love, so grand, eternal,
  We would thank Thee, O our King.

—Selected.

THANKSGIVING.

Lord, for the erring thought,
Not into evil wrought;
Lord, for the wicked will,
Betrayed and baffled still;
For the heart from itself kept,
Our thanksgiving accept.

For ignorant hopes that were
Broken to our blind prayer;
For pain, death, sorrow, sent
Unto our chastisement;
For all loss of seeming good,
Quicken our gratitude.
—Howells.

TO WHOM SHALL WE GIVE THANKS?

A little boy had sought the pump
From whence the sparkling water burst,
And drank with eager joy the draught
That kindly quenched his raging thirst;
Then gracefully he touch'd his cap—
"I thank you, Mr. Pump," he said,
"For this nice drink you've given me!"
(This little boy had been well bred.)

Then said the Pump, "My little man,
You're welcome to what I have done;
But I am not the one to thank—
I only help the water run."
"O, then," the little fellow said,
(Polite he always meant to be!)
"Cold Water, please accept my thanks;
You have been very kind to me."

"Ah!" said Cold Water, "don't thank me;
 Far up the hillside lives the Spring
 That sends me forth with generous hand
 To gladden every living thing."
"I'll thank the Spring, then," said the boy,
 And gracefully he bowed his head.
"O, don't thank me, my little man,"
 The Spring with silvery accents said—

"O, don't thank me, for what am I
 Without the dew and summer rain?
 Without their aid I ne'er could quench
 Your thirst, my little boy, again."
"O, well, then," said the little boy,
 "I'll gladly thank the Rain and Dew."
"Pray, don't thank us; without the Sun
 We could not fill one cup for you."

"Then, Mr. Sun, ten thousand thanks
 For all that you have done for me."
"Stop!" said the Sun, with blushing face;
 "My little fellow, don't thank me;
 'Twas from the ocean's mighty stores
 I drew the draught I gave to thee."
"O, Ocean, thanks, then," said the boy;
 It echo'd back, "Not unto me—

"Not unto me; but unto Him
 Who formed the depths in which I lie;
 Go give thy thanks, my little boy,
 To Him who will thy wants supply."

The boy took off his cap, and said,
In tones so gentle and subdued,
"O God, I thank Thee for this gift;
Thou art the Giver of all good."
—Anon.

HARVEST HYMN.

Once more the liberal year laughs out
O'er richer stores than gems of gold;
Once more with harvest song and shout
Is nature's boldest triumph told.

Oh, favors old, yet ever new;
Oh, blessings with the sunshine sent.
The bounty overruns our due,
The fullness shames our discontent.

Who murmurs at his lot to-day?
Who scorns his native fruit and bloom,
Or sighs for dainties far away,
Besides the bounteous board of home?

Thank heaven, instead, that Freedom's arm
Can change a rocky soil to gold;
And brave and generous lives can warm
A clime with northern ices cold.

And by these altars wreathed with flowers,
And fields with fruits awake again,
Thanksgiving for the golden hours,
The earlier and the latter rain.
—Whittier.

THE PUMPKIN.

O greenly and fair, in the lands of the sun,
The rivers of the gourd and the rich melon run;
And the rock, and the tree, and the cottage unfold
With broad leaves all greenness, and blossoms all gold,
Like that which o'er Nineveh's prophet once grew,
While he waited to know that his warning was true,
And longed for the stormcloud, and listened in vain
For the rush of the whirlwind and the red-fire rain.

On the banks of the Xenil, the dark Spanish maiden
Comes up with the fruit of the tangled vine laden;
And the Creole of Cuba laughs out to behold
Though orange leaves shining the broad spheres of gold;
Yet, with dearer delight from his home in the North,
On the fields of his harvest the Yankee looks forth
Where crook-necks are coiling and yellow fruit shines
And the sun of September melts down on his vines.

Ah! on Thanksgiving Day, when from East and from West,
From North and from South come the pilgrim and guest,
When the gray-haired New Englander sees, 'round his board,
The old, broken links of affection restored;
When the care-wearied man seeks his mother once more,
And the worn matron smiled where the girl smiled before,
What moistened the lip and what dampened the eye?
What calls back the past like the rich pumpkin pie?

O, fruit loved of boyhood!—the old days recalling!
When wood grapes were purpling and brown nuts were falling!
When wild, ugly faces we carved in its skin,
Glaring out through the dark with a candle within!
When we laughed round the cornheap with hearts all in tune—
Our chair a broad pumpkin—our lantern the moon.
Telling tales of the fairy who traveled, like steam,
In a pumpkin-shell coach with two rats for her team!

Then thanks for thy present! None sweeter or better
E'er smoked from an oven, or circled a platter!
Fairer hands never wrought at a pastry more fine,
Brighter eyes never watched over its baking than thine.
And the prayer which my heart is too full to express
Swells my heart that thy shadow may never be less.
That the days of thy lot may be lengthened below
And the fame of thy worth like a pumpkin-vine grow!
And thy life be as sweet, and its last sunset sky,
Golden tinted and fair as thine own pumpkin pie!
—Whittier.

The summer grains are harvested; the stubble-fields are dry,
Where June winds rolled. in light and shade, the pale-green
    waves of rye;
But still, on gentle hill-slopes, in valleys fringed with wood,
Ungathered, bleaching in the sun, the heavy corn-crop stood.

Bent low by autumn's wind and rain, through husks that, dry
    and sere,
Unfolded from their ripened charge, shone out the yellow ear;

Beneath, the turnip lay concealed, in many a verdant fold,
And glistened in the slanting light the pumpkin's sphere of
    gold.

There wrought the busy harvesters; and many a creaking wain
Bore slowly to the long barn floor its load of husk and grain;
Till broad and red, as when he rose, the sun sank down at last,
And like a merry guest's farewell, the day in brightness passed.
           —Whittier. ("Popular Educator.")

A THANKSGIVING TREASURE.

We planted the seed in a well-spaded garden;
  We covered it over with earth soft and warm,
And watched every day for the first tender leaflets,
  Then carefully guarded and kept them from harm.

The kind summer sun sent his warmth to our treasure,
  Which put forth new leaves as he lighted the way;
The rain and the dew gave it drink when it thirsted,
  And thus it grew stronger and larger each day.

Then a bud from the stem raised its head, one bright morning,
  And slowly unfolded to greet the warm day;
It nodded and smiled at the green leaves about it,
  Then folded its petals and faded away.

Where the blossom had grown we discovered a something,
  'Twas green and so hard it seemed almost like wood,
But grandfather smiled at our questions and answered,
  "The cane turns to sugar when children are good."

The green ball grew large as the evenings grew longer,
  And then, as Jack Frost brought the first thought of cold,
The green ball turned yellow. It shone in the garden
  As round as the sun and as yellow as gold.

A bright happy day to our land is soon coming
  And grandfather says to be good we must try,
So the cane may turn into the sweetest of sugar—
  Our hard yellow ball to a Thanksgiving pie.
        —By Cora J. Alberger, in "Popular Educator."

THANKSGIVING JOYS.

Cartloads of pumpkins as yellow as gold,
Onions in silvery strings,
Shining red apples and clusters of grapes,
Nuts, and a host of good things,
Chickens and turkeys and little fat pigs—
These are what Thanksgiving brings.
Work is forgotten and play-time begins;
From office and schoolroom and hall;
Fathers and mothers and uncles and aunts,
Nieces and nephews, and all
Speed away home, as they hear from afar
The voice of old Thanksgiving call.
Now is the time to forget all your cares,
Cast every trouble away;
Think of your blessings, remember your joys,
Don't be afraid to be gay.
None are too old and none are too young
To frolic on Thanksgiving day.
        —"Youth's Companion."

HIS GOLDEN CORN.

Heap high the farmer's wintry hoard!
Heap high the golden corn!
The richer gifts has autumn poured
From out her lavish horn!
Let other lands, exulting, glean
The apple from the pine,
The orange from its glossy green,
The cluster from the vine.

We better love the hardy gift
Our rugged vales bestow,
To cheer us when the storm shall drift
Our harvest-fields with snow.
But let the good old crop adorn
The hills our fathers trod;
Still let us for His golden corn
Send up our thanks to God.
—Selected.

THANKSGIVING DAY.

Over the river and through the wood,
  To grandfather's house we go,
The horse knows the way to carry the sleigh
  Through the white and drifted snow.

Over the river and through the wood,
   Oh, how the wind does blow!
It stings the toes and bites the nose,
   As over the ground we go.

Over the river and through the wood,
   Trot fast, my dapple-gray!
Spring over the ground like a hunting hound,
   For this is Thanksgiving day.

Over the river and through the wood,
   And straight through the barnyard gate;
We seem to go extremely slow—
   It is so hard to wait!

Over the river and through the wood,
   Now Grandmother's cap I spy,
Hurrah for the fun! Is the pudding done?
   Hurrah for the pumpkin pie!
        —L. M. Childs. ("Popular Educator.")

GRANDMA'S PUMPKIN PIES.

My mother's pies are very good
   For common days, but O, my eyes!
You ought to be at Grandma Gray's,
Where we all go Thanksgiving days,
   And taste of Grandma's pumpkin pies.

The aunts and uncles all are there,
   And cousins, too, of every size;
And when the turkey's "had his day,"
And Grandma's pudding's stowed away,
   Then next will come the pumpkin pies.

Oh, apple pie is very good,
   And chocolate, cream, and mince, likewise;
But if you knew my Grandma Gray
And tried her cooking, you would say,
   Hurrah for Grandma's pumpkin pies!
               —"Popular Educator."

OUT FOR A WALK.

A Jack-o'-lantern went for a walk
   With a turkey gobbler gay.
The time they chose for their promenade
   Was the night of Thanksgiving Day.
Said the Jack-o'-lantern, "Let us go
   And into the window peep,
Where Billy Boy, tired out at last,
   Is lying fast asleep."

On tip-toe, then, up the hill they stole—
   "We'll frighten him well," said they;
"Then he'll not want to eat all our brothers up
   On next Thanksgiving Day."
"Gobble, gobble!" then cried the gobbler gay,
   And Billy woke at the sound;
He sat up in bed and rubbed his eyes,
   And began to look around.

But when he saw the grinning face,
    And the bird with bristling wings,
He thought of witches and brownies and imps,
    And all those kind of things.
And he gave a scream and hid his face,
    And his mother soon was near.
"What is the matter, my son?" she said.
    "You are feeling ill, I fear."

"They are after me! They are after me!"
    Cried Billy with streaming eye;
"You are dreaming," his mother said. "You've had
    Too much turkey and pumpkin pie!"
But the Jack-o'-lantern grinned with glee,
    And whispered, "Now, come away,
We'll stay out all night and find all the boys
    Who've eaten too much to-day."
—L. F. Armitage in "American Primary Teacher."

A BOY'S OPINION.

Oh, Valentine day is well enough,
    And Fourth of July is jolly,
And Christmas time is beautiful,
    With its gifts and wreaths of holly;
New Year's calling is rather nice,
    And Hallowe'en sports are funny,
And a May-day party isn't bad
    When the weather is warm and sunny.

Oh, all of them are well enough;
   But the day that is best worth living
Is when we all go to grandmamma's
   To a splendid big Thanksgiving.

                    —Emma C. Dowd.

THANKSGIVING LETTER.

A letter once poor Katie wrote,
   And on its way it sped
One bright Thanksgiving morning.
   'Twas thus the letter read:

"O farmer man! O farmer man!
   Do please to come this way,
Because we want a turkey
   On this Thanksgiving Day.
O, do you think that none of us
   Here in this narrow lane
Have nothing to be thankful for,
   In spite of toil and pain?
I have two hands with which to work,
   Two feet with which to walk,
And I can hear, and I can speak,
   And with my mama talk.
And when I am cold and hungry,
   I then can sing a song
And think I'm warm. When headaches come,
   They never do last long.

With so much to be thankful for,
   I'd keep Thanksgiving Day;
So bring a turkey, and some time
   You'll surely get your pay.
Leave it at Bragg's Lane, number five,
   And please wait for my thanks."
And the postman gave this letter
   To crabbed Farmer Hanks,

Who hung his biggest turkey
   That day on Katie's door.
With it this note: "You've made me, child,
   More thankful than before."
—Ed. Gazette.

RECITATION FOR THE LITTLE FOLKS.

Little songs, all full of joy, little lips can sing;
Little voices, soft and sweet, may their tribute bring;
Little verses can express what we wish to tell
Of a loving care that keeps what little folks so well.

Kindly on us little ones beams a Father's smile;
Tender care and watchfulness guard us all the while;
For the pleasant things we have, clothing, shelter, food,
We would, in our happy songs, show our gratitude.
—Selected.

WHICH?

Two little old ladies, one grave, one gay,
In the selfsame cottage lived day by day;
One could not be happy, "Because," she said,
"So many children were hungry for bread."
And she really had not the heart to smile
When the world was so wicked all the while.
The other old lady smiled all day long,
As she knitted or sewed or crooned a song;
She had not time to be sad, she said,
When hungry children were crying for bread;
So she baked and knitted and gave away,
And declared the world grew better each day.
Two little old ladies, one grave, one gay;
Now, which do you think chose the wiser way?
—St. Nicholas.

THANKSGIVING.

The ripe, rosy apples are all gathered in;
They wait for the winter in barrel and bin;
And nuts for the children, a plentiful store,
Are spread out to dry on the broad attic floor;
The great golden pumpkins, that grew such a size,
Are ready to make into Thanksgiving pies;
And all the good times that the children hold dear
Have come around again with the feast of the year.

Now, what shall we do in our bright, happy homes
To welcome this time of good times as it comes?
And what do you say is the very best way
To show we are grateful on Thanksgiving Day?
The best thing that hearts that are thankful can do
Is this: to make thankful some other hearts, too;
For lives that are grateful, and sunny and glad,
To carry their sunshine to lives that are sad;
For children who have all they want and to spare,
Their good things with poor little children to share;
For this will bring blessing and this is the way
To show we are thankful on Thanksgiving Day.
—Selected.

JOHN WHITE'S THANKSGIVING.

"Thanksgiving! for what?"
    And he muttered a curse—
"For the plainest of food
    And an empty purse;
For a life of hard work
    And the shabbiest clothes?
But it's idle to talk
    Of a poor man's woes.
Let the rich give thanks;
    It is they who can—
There is nothing in life
    For a laboring man."

So said John White
  To his good wife Jane,
And o'er her face
  Stole a look of pain.
"Nothing, dear John?"
  And he thought again;
Then glanced more kindly
  Down on Jane.
"I was wrong," he said;
  "I'd forgotten you;
And I've my health
  And the baby, too."

And the baby crowed—
  'Twas a bouncing boy—
And o'er Jane's face
  Came a look of joy;
And she kissed her John
  As he went away;
And he said to himself,
  As he worked that day:
"I was wrong, very wrong;
  I'll not grumble again;
I should be thankful
  For baby and Jane."

—Selected.

THAT THINGS ARE NO WORSE, SIRE.

From the time of our old Revolution,
   When we threw off the yoke of the King,
Has descended this phrase to remember,
   To remember, to say, and to sing;
'Tis a phrase that is full of a lesson;
   It can comfort and warm like a fire;
It can cheer us when days are the darkest:
   "That things are no worse, O my sire."

'Twas King George's prime minister said it,
   To the king, who had questioned, in heat,
What he meant by appointing Thanksgiving
   In such days of ill-luck and defeat;
"What's the cause of your day of Thanksgiving?
   Tell me, pray," cried the king in his ire.
Said the minister, "This is the reason—
   That things are no worse, O my sire."

There has nothing come down, in the story,
   Of the answer returned by the king.
But I think on his throne he sat silent,
   And confessed it a sensible thing;
For there's never a burden so heavy
   That it might not be heavier still;
There is never so bitter a sorrow
   That the cup could not fuller fill.

And what of care and of sadness
  Our life and our duties may bring,
There's always the cause for Thanksgiving
  Which the minister told to the king.
'Tis a lesson to sing and to remember;
  It can comfort and warm like a fire,
Can cheer us when days are the darkest,
  "That things are no worse, O my sire."
                    —Helen Hunt Jackson.

THE PURITAN'S THANKSGIVING.

"Why do they keep Thanksgiving?"
  Asked Golden-hair of me,
  As in the twilight shadows
  She sat beside my knee;
"Why does it come in winter,
  When days are dark and cold,
  And not when summer's sunshine
  Is pouring floods of gold?"

I brush from her snowy forehead
  The shining waves of hair,
  For she is bright and bonny,
  With not a thought of care;
"If Golden-hair will listen,
  I'll tell the reason why
  The people keep Thanksgiving
  Under a wintry sky.

"Long, long ago, my darling,
 When the country here was new,
There sailed across the ocean
 A good ship, strong and true;
She brought brave men and women,
 Who toiled with heart and hand
To build their household altars
 Within the strange, new land.

"All day in the fragrant forest
 The settlers felled the trees,
And the ringing sound of axes
 Was borne upon the breeze;
And far within the clearings
 Their humble homes were made,
Where birds sang in the thickets
 And streams of water played.

"But once there came a summer
 With storms of sleet and snow
That froze the tender branches,
 And laid the young crops low;
The men toiled, worn and weary,
 All day in the barren field,
But the harvest brought them only
 A small and scanty yield.

"And faith began to waver,
 And the women prayed and wept,
For the children must be nourished
 With the small supplies they kept;

Until one day the preacher,
His kind face lined with care,
Had called his flock together
To meet, and offer prayer.

"But hark! a sudden clamor
Has risen in the town;
And look! within the harbor
A ship sails slowly down
Over the dancing water,
Over the crested wave—
They know that she brings them plenty
To help, sustain, and save.

"And far from over the water
There sounds a ringing cheer,
And then, before they answer,
Another, loud and clear:
And loosened from their moorings,
The boats have sailed away,
While the gallant ship has anchored
In the shelter of the bay.

"Rich are the stores she brings them
Of welcome food and wine;
And hands are clasped in greeting,
And joyous faces shine;
There is warmth and hope in future,
There is corn in golden store
To last till cold is ended,
And the summer comes once more.

"'God bless our friends in England!'
  The gray-haired preacher said,
  As on the sands the people
  Knelt with uncovered head.
'We thank the God who leads us
  By many winding ways,
  And changed our supplications
  To joyful songs of praise.'

"And this is why, my darling,
  In the fading of the year,
  When the yellow moon is shining,
  And nights are cold and clear;
When purple grapes have ripened,
  And autumn brought its hoard,
  We call our friends together
  Around the festal board."

God bless our brave New England!
  Her hills in grandeur rise;
  Her storms are fierce and raging,
  But blue her smiling skies;
Proud are her sons and daughters,
  Who own her noble sway,
  Of the grand old pilgrim fathers
  Who kept Thanksgiving Day.
          —Arthur's Home Magazine.

AMONG THE APPLES.

Red, and russet, and yellow,
  Lying here in a heap—
Pippins rounded and mellow;
  Greenings for winter keep;
Seek-no-furthers, whose blushing
  The soul of a saint would try,
Till his face showed the crimson flushing
  The cheek of a northern spy.

Hid from the winter weather,
  Safe from the wind and sleet,
Here in a pile together
  Russet and pippin meet.
And in this dim and dusty
  Old cellar they fondly hold
A breath like the grapes made musty
  By the summer's radiant gold.

Each seems to hold a vagrant
  Sunbeam lost from the sky,
When lily blooms were fragrant
  Walls for the butterfly;
And when the snow was flying,
  What feast in the hoarded store
Of crimson and yellow lying
  Heaped high on the sandy floor!

Fruitage of bright spring splendor,
  Of leaf and blossom-time,
That no tropic land can lend, or
  Take from this frosty clime—
Fruit for the hearthstone meeting,
  Whose flavor naught can destroy,
How you make my heart's swift beating
  Throb with the pulse of a boy!

Apples, scarlet and golden,
  Apples, juicy and tart,
Bringing again the olden
  Joy to the weary heart.
You send the swift thoughts sweeping
  Through wreckage of time and tears,
To that hidden chamber keeping
  The gladness of youth's bright years.
                —T. S. Collier.

THE CAT'S THANKSGIVING SOLILOQUY.

I'm just about tired of waiting
  For my Thanksgiving treat;
I see them about the table,
  And they eat, and eat, and eat.
They do not think of poor pussy,
  Who has had so long to wait;
Why doesn't some one remember
  That it's grown very late?

And haven't I smelt that turkey
   Since into the oven it went?
If they'd give me just one drumstick,
   Why, then, I'd be content.
But, no! they sit there talking
   And laughing aloud with glee;
I wish that some one among them
   Would throw down a bone to me.
There's that greedy little Teddy,
   Three times he's passed his plate,
And that turkey's growing smaller
   At a very rapid rate;
And see Jack's face! 'Tis shining
   With gravy up to his eyes.
I wonder they take no notice
   When they hear my hungry cries.
Oh, dear! there's dessert to follow,
   The pudding and pumpkin pies,
And the fruit and nuts and candy,
   And, oh, how fast time flies!
Ah, there's gentle little Ethel,
   She's so loving and so kind,
She's bringing me some turkey bones,
   And a grateful cat she'll find.

—L. F. Armitage.

THE ORPHAN TURKEYS.

(A true story.)

Twenty-two little turkeys
  Were hatched by two hens,
And, one by one, some of them
  Came to bad ends;

Till only six turkeys
  Were shivering with cold.
The old hens had weaned them
  When scarce a month old.

And, now, when the rain comes,
  Oh, where can they go—
Each disconsolate turkey,
  The picture of woe?

It was time for a venture,
  So the poor little things
Crept up for a shelter
  'Neath the old rooster's wings.

That old Brahma rooster
  Didn't say, "What a fix!"
But, with his broad wings,
  He sheltered all six.

And not only then,
   But the next rainy day,
He sheltered them all
   In the same friendly way.

The farmer's wife saw it,
   And said, "I declare,
Kind-hearted old fellow!
   Your life I will spare.

"I fully intended
   To take off your head;
But those two old hens
   Shall lose theirs instead."

My dear little children,
   You always will find,
With folks or with fowls,
   It pays to be kind.
—Mrs. H. E. Jenkins, in "Our Little Ones, and the Nursery."

LITTLE NUT PEOPLE.

(Have each pupil reciting hold in his hand the nut about which he speaks. He should hold it up to view as he recites.)

(Chestnut:)
   Old Mistress Chestnut once lived in a burr
   Padded and lined with the softest of fur.
   Jack Frost split it wide, with his keen silver knife,
   And tumbled her out at the risk of her life.

(Almond:)
>   Here is Don Almond, a grandee from Spain,
>   Some raisins from Malaga came in his train.
>   He has a twin brother a shade or two leaner;
>   When both come together, we shout, "Philopena!"

(Walnut:)
>   Here is Sir Walnut; he's English, you know,
>   A friend of my Lady and Lord So-and-So.
>   Whenever you ask old Sir Walnut to dinner,
>   Be sure to make much of the gouty old sinner.

(Peanut:)
>   Little Miss Peanut, from North Carolina,
>   She's not 'ristocratic, but no nut is finer.
>   Sometimes she is roasted and burnt to a cinder;
>   In Georgia they call her Miss Goober or Pindar.

(Hazelnut:)
>   Little Miss Hazelnut; in her best bonnet,
>   Is lovely enough to be put in a sonnet;
>   And young Mr. Filbert has journeyed from Kent,
>   To ask her to marry him soon after Lent.

(Hickory:)
>   There is old Hickory; look at him well.
>   A general was named for him, so I've heard tell.
>   Take care how you hit him! He sometimes hits back!
>   This stolid old chap is a hard nut to crack.

(Butternut:)
>   Old Mr. Butternut, just from Brazil,
>   Is rugged and rough as the side of a hill;
>   But, like many a countenance quite as ill-favored,
>   His covers a kernel deliciously flavored .

(Pecan:)
>Here is a southerner, graceful and slim,
>In flavor no nut is quite equal to him.
>Ha, Monsieur Pecan, you know what it means
>To be served with black coffee in French New Orleans.

(All:)
>And, now, dear schoolmates, I'm sure we have told
>All the queer rhymes that a nutshell can hold.
>
>—Selected.

THE LITTLE PILGRIM MAID.

(Recitations, with motions.)

There was a little pilgrim maid,
    Who used to sit up so; (1)
I wonder if she ever laughed
    Two hundred years ago.

She wore such funny little mitts, (2)
    And dainty cap of silk. (3)
She had a little porringer
    For her brown bread and milk.

She was so good—so very good—
    Ah, me, I most despair; (4)
She never tore her Sabbath dress (5)
    A-sliding down the stair.

But, then, I really try, and try
    To do the best I can; (6)
P'r'aps I (7) can be almost as good
    As little Puritan.

And if, when next Thanksgiving comes,
 I try to sit up so, (8)
 Maybe I'll seem from Pilgrim land
 Two hundred years ago.

(Motions: (1) Hands folded in a prim manner, body erect; (2) hands held up to show mitts; (3) point to cap; (4) gesture of despair; (5) dress held out at sides; (6) hands folded; (7) point to self; (8) prim position, same as (1).)

—Primary Education.

ELSIE'S THANKSGIVING.

(Recitation for a little girl holding doll.)

Dolly, it's almost Thanksgiving. Do you know what I mean, my dear?
No? Well, I couldn't expect it; you haven't been with us a year.
And you came with my auntie from Paris, far over the wide blue sea;
And you'll keep your first Thanksgiving, my beautiful dolly, with me.
I'll tell you about it, my darling; for grandma's explained it all,
So that I understand why Thanksgiving always comes late in the fall,
When the nuts and the apples are gathered, and the work in the fields is done,
And the fields, all reaped and silent, are asleep in the autumn sun.

It is then that we praise our Father, who sends the rain and
    the dew,
Whose wonderful loving-kindness is every morning new.
Unless we'd be heathen, dolly, or worse, we must sing and pray,
And think about good things, dolly, when we keep Thanks-
    giving Day.
But I like it very much better when from church we all go
    home,
And the married brothers and sisters, and the troops of cous-
    ins come,
And we're ever so long at the table, and dance and shout and
    play,
In the merry evening, dolly, that ends Thanksgiving Day.
    —Margaret E. Sangster. ("Primary Education.")

A MOTHER GOOSE ENTERTAINMENT.

(As a portion of a school entertainment, the following sketch of Mother Goose was recited by a little girl, and the tableaux of Jack Horner, Boy Blue, Miss Muffet, Little Bo Peep, and the "Bachelor who lived by himself," were given. Jack Horner's pie had a crust of manila paper over a huge dish, and the plum was a big prune. Boy Blue's haystack consisted of an armful of hay covering an overturned chair. In the first scene he was fast asleep; in the second, he was standing up, blowing his horn. Miss Muffet's spider, suspended by a thread, was yellow, and large enough for anybody to see. The "Bachelor" required four scenes: First, he was sitting by the shelf of bread and cheese, darning a stocking; second, he was on his way to London, with all his worldly possessions tied up in a handkerchief, slung on a stick over his shoulder; third, he had the little wife in a wheelbarrow; fourth, the wheelbarrow was upset, and the husband and wife both looked very much surprised. Before each tableau the rhyme illustrated was recited by a little boy or girl.)

In the days of the Pilgrim mothers,
   When children's books were few,
A kind and loving grandma
   Sang ditties, old and new.

She sang them over and over,
   While the children laughed with glee,
And all the babies who heard them
   Were happy as they could be.

The father of one of the babies,
   Whose cheeks with laughter shook,
Wrote down the rhymes as he heard them,
   And made them into a book.

Thousands and thousands of copies
   Have been printed and sold since then,
And, as fast as the babies keep coming,
   They're printed and sold again.

The face of the quaint old singer
   Was painted long years ago;
In the Old South Church, in Boston,
   Her portrait is hanging, you know.

The name of this grandma so jolly
  Was Madam Elizabeth Goose;
And, like other famous women,
  She has had her share of abuse.

Folks say that her rhymes are silly,
  That they do not teach the truth,
And that nothing so full of nonsense
  Should be taught to the modern youth;

For this is an age of science,
  And fairies have had their day;
But facts are often tiresome,
  And workers must sometimes play.

Then give to the older children
  Golden thoughts and gems for use,
But let the babies have the rhymes
  Of dear old Mother Goose.
      —Elizabeth Lloyd, in "The Primary School."

THE TEN LITTLE INDIANS.

(To be most effective this play should be presented by boys under ten years of age. At the close of each speech Indian songs may be sung by one or all of the ten little Indians.)

Curtains and stage effects are not necessary. The schoolroom may be decorated with Indian relics. Class collections of Indian pictures and specimens of children's daily work in clay, sand, weaving, drawing, story-writing, etc., may be on exhibition.

The "Ten Little Indians," in costume, march, to the sound of the piano or other music, from a side room to the rear of the platform, where they arrange themselves in a line. Each then steps forward, makes his speech, and returns to place. When they have finished, all march out to the sound of music.)

Costume of Massasoit: Blouse, kilt, and leggins made of yellow felt, decorated with beads; belt and moccasins, made of buckskin; wig, made of long, coarse, black hair parted in the middle; cap of turkey feathers; burnt umber, used to give the dark, swarthy complexion needed.

Costume of Natches Winnemucca: Red hunting suit, open at neck; beaded belt, beaded powder pouch, red and yellow blanket, an old gun, chains and bracelet, braided wig, decorated with shells and feathers; red and brown "grease paint" used for greasing the face.

Costume of Powhatan: Moccasins and tan stockings, red apron, extending from the neck to the knees; colored blanket, draped over the body, leaving the red apron showning in front; head-dress, red band and feathers; face darkened with burnt umber.

Costume of Sitting Bull: Tan cloth jacket, trimmed with beads and feathers, extending to the knees; tan leggins, fringed with brown; very large and conspicuous head-dress, with row of feathers extending almost to the middle of back; war paint; tomahawk.

Costume of Pontiac: Red shirt, open at the neck; buff leggins, fringed with red; red and black blanket, braided wig, war bonnet, made of feathers; pipe of peace, many strings of beads; brown umber for face.

Costume of Black Hawk: Brown felt hunting suit, buckskin belt and moccasins, red and black blanket, large head-dress of turkey feathers; wampum, bow and arrows.

Costume of Tecumseh: Tan felt suit, trimmed in feathers; buckskin moccasins, large brown blanket, draped at side; head-dress of turkey feathers, quiver filled with arrows, wampum; umber for face.

Costume of Philip: Brown, tight-fitting suit, red blanket, moccasins, wig, parted in middle; gun, hatchet, war-paint.

Carlos Montezuma: Street suit, long overcoat, broad hat, gloves; wig of short hair, parted on the side; physician's medicine case.

Costume of Hiawatha: Brown sweater, tan skirt fringed with brown, beaded belt, tan leggins; wig, long, loose hair; head-dress, band with feathers in front; strings of wampum wound around the neck, bow and quiver of arrows.

(Massasoit:)

"Welcome, Englishmen! Welcome, Englishmen!" I was the first Indian chief to send this message to the palefaces, who called themselves the Plymouth Colony. My name is Massasoit. The great King Philip was once my little pappoose.

My tribe, the Wanpanoags, call me the "Great Commander of the Country." I like the palefaces. I smoked the pipe of peace with them when they first came to America. I was always their friend. When I went to the "Happy Hunting Ground" they named the great spring in Rhode Island "Massasoit." Palefaces, I thank you!

—Elvira Johnson.

(Natches Winnemucca:)

I am the good chief, Natches Winnemucca. My people are the Piutes, and we live in Nevada.

Once, long ago, the Bannocks, and some other fierce Indians, made war against the white people. I would not join them, so they took me and my sons captive. The brave Sarah Winnemucca rescued us.

After the war was over, Sarah wrote a book telling about it. If you read her book, you will learn more about Natches and his people.

I am an old chief now; I can no longer hunt and dance. I sit by the fire and watch the young braves dance, and listen to their songs. —Alma Plumb.

(Powhatan:)

Greetings, palefaces! greetings, chiefs! I come from the forests of Virginia, and my name is Powhatan. I am ruler over a mighty tribe.

Once all the lands, far and near, was our hunting ground, and no other tribe dared cross our path. Then we lived happily; but the white man came, and since then we have had no peace. The guns of the white man shoot far, but the Indian knows how to lie in wait in a dark thicket and surprise the enemy. He can also surprise the wild animals of the forest. He often creeps near the timid deer, but so quietly that it does not suspect his presence until, too late, it hears the whirr of the fatal arrow.

You have all heard of my daughter Pocahontas. She is a brave girl and a worthy daughter of the chief.

Once Captain John Smith was my prisoner, and I meant to kill him. Pocahontas was his friend, and begged me to spare his life, so I set him free. The palefaces told Pocahontas to come to their homes to visit them. She went often. When she grew older she married an Englishman named John Rolf. She went to England, where King James and all his court admired and praised her. They called her "Lady Rebecca."

—Edith Edwards.

(Sitting Bull:)

Behold the dreaded foe of the white man. My name is Sitting Bull. I lived in the present century, and was chief of the powerful Sioux tribe that lived in North Dakota.

Not many years ago, when some of you were little boys and girls going to school, there lived an old chief who preached a queer doctrine. He taught that there would be a great upheaval of nations; every paleface would suddenly be swept from the face of the earth, and the blood of eighty millions would pay for the wrongs done the red men.

I believed this same doctrine, and preached it to my tribes. They became so much excited over this belief that many of them were about to cause great trouble and bloodshed. The United States sent General Miles and several hundred soldiers up there to stop these troubles. One day they captured me, and were going to take me away prisoner. My comrades fought hard to get me back, and during this terrible battle I and my son, and a number of my comrades, were shot and killed.

—E. E. Hough.

(Pontiac:)

I am bold Pontiac, chief of the Ottawas. In 1746 I and my children of the forest defended the French at Detroit against an attack by some northern tribes.

When I found that the French had been driven from Canada I agreed to the surrender of Detroit and persuaded several hundred Indians to give up their design of cutting off the English. I felt all the time that the English hated me and my people, so I planned to exterminate them and take Detroit, but my plans were disclosed and the garrison was prepared when I arrived.

Later I surrounded Detroit, but failed to take it. The English then planned an attack, but the Canadians told me about it, and when the English had advanced near enough, my men opened fire upon them. This fight was known as the battle of Bloody Bridge.

Although I failed in my main plot of cutting off the whites, yet I captured eight garrisons and desolated some of the most fertile valleys on the frontier. The English finally succeeded in quieting most of the tribes, so a meeting was held and several of us Indian chiefs concluded a treaty of peace with the white men.

—Louise Grozelier.

(Black Hawk:)

Do you see this old man before you? I am Black Hawk, chief of the Sacs and Foxes, Indian tribes of Illinois.

Many years ago, when Columbus came to America, we owned all this great country. When I was a boy I did not live so far west, but now white people own the home of my fathers.

Two centuries ago the smoke of our wigwams and the fires of our councils rose in every valley from Hudson's bay to farthest Florida, from the Atlantic ocean to the Mississippi and the Great Lakes. The whistle of our arrows and the deadly tomahawks startled the wild animals in the forests. But now we have few forests. When the white men come they cut down the trees. At their approach the deer leaves the forest and the opossum and beaver flee. When the forests are cut down our springs dry up.

The whites with their hordes of men drove us from our homes. Black Hawk tried to save his nation, but I and my warriors were taken prisoners. We were taken to Washington. I talked with President Jackson. I liked him. We were taken to Fortress Monroe, Virginia, and to other great cities. The whites gave us good counsel. We gave all up to the white men.

I fought for my village, but it is yours now. I was once a great warrior; a few snows ago I was fighting against the whites. Perhaps that was wrong—but that is past. I am done.

—Lena Kelley.

(Tecumseh:)

Behold Tecumseh, chief of the Shawnee Indians! My brother was a prophet. Nearly a hundred years ago, when your grandfathers were little boys, my brother and I tried to gather all the tribes of the west into one large army to drive the white people out of our land.

But one day, while I was away, one of your great generals marched his army into the city and defeated all the Indians.

A few year later, when war broke out between America and England, I and my men helped the English. We went up north into Canada and joined their army. I was made a brigadier-general and commanded large numbers of soldiers; but one day in the terrible battle of the Thames I was shot and killed.

—F. T. Bailey.

(King Philip:)

Before you stands the great King Philip. I am not a friend to the whites as my father, Massasoit, was. My name was given to me by the white men, and I am proud of it.

We sold all our lands to the white men for these blankets, hatchets, and guns; but now we want more. They have made cornfields of our hunting grounds. What are we to live on? We have no place to hunt deer.

My home was on yonder Mount Hope. From my wigwam I could overlook all the country and rule my tribe. Now I have been driven from there, my cattle have been taken and my corn burned. I must have revenge; we shall go to war with these palefaces. Philip is a big Indian. He can regain his lost hunting ground.

Alas, for King Philip! Other Indians joined the palefaces and his brave tribes were crushed.

—Elena Broderick.

(Carlos Montezuma:)

I am an Apache Indian, and my name is Carlos Montezuma. When I was four years old the Pima Indians sold me to a white man for thirty dollars.

For many years my home was in Chicago. I clerked in a drugstore in that city for several years. I then went to the University of Chicago, and obtained a medical diploma.

I have acted as physician on several of the agencies; was head physician at Carlisle, and am now in business for myself in Chicago.

—Edna Hyde.

(Hiawatha:)

I am Hiawatha. Longfellow has written a beautiful poem about me. My grandmother was old Nikomis. She rocked me to sleep in a linden cradle, and this is the song she sang to me:

"E-wa-yea! my little ow-let,
Who is this that lights the wigwam,
With his great eyes lights the wigwam?
E-wa-yea! my little ow-let."

(The music of this song can be found in the collection by Elizabeth U. Emerson and Kate L. Brown, published by Oliver Ditson Company.

When they can be obtained, Indian songs may be sung by each or all of the Ten Little Indians at the close of each speech. In some of the old readers there are the speeches of Red Jacket, Gehale, and other chiefs. These, recited in costume, add much to the interest of an Indian entertainment. The recitation, "Hiawatha's Childhood," with tableaux, is also a pleasing and instructive feature.)

SONGS

"Merry Christmas Has Come," "Christmas Waltz Song," "Christmas Carol," "Christmas Song," "Carol" ("Christmas Chimes"), in "Kindergarten Chimes." Boards, $1.25

"O, Clap, Clap the Hands," in "Finger Plays," by Emilie Poulsson.

"Jolly Old Saint Nicholas," in "Songs, Games and Rhymes" ....Paper, $1.25

"Christmas is Coming," "Christmas Greeting," "Hark! the Bells Are Ringing," "Dear Santa, Now Appear," in "Merry Songs and Games" (Clara Beeson Hubbard).

Excellent Thanksgiving and Christmas Songs in "Songs and Games for Little Ones," by Gertrude Walker and Harriet Jenks.

"The Song Series" (Sacred Songs for Children), by Eudora Lucas Hailmann.

"Waken, Little Children," and Christmas Hymn, in "Songs for Little Children," by Eleanor Smith.

"Blessings on Effort," "Thanksgiving Song," "Christmas Lullaby," "Christmas Night," "Christmas Star," "Presentation Song," "The Song of Christ," in "Song Stories for the Kindergarten." by Mildred J. and Patty S. Hill. $1.00

"Columbia," a National Anthem (for Thanksgiving), founded on the History of America.................. .12

"Our King Emmanuel," a Service of Scripture and Song for Christmas for the Church, by Emma Pitt.... .95

"The Morning Star" (for the Church), a short Christmas Cantata of Service, by Asa Hull................. .05

"Harvest Home," "Christmas-tide," in "Songs for Children.".. .10

"The Child's American Hymn," by G. W. Chadwick, in "Children's Souvenir Song Book" (advanced collection of beautiful songs).

"Hail, Old Father Christmas," in "Christmas Carols" (contains twelve excellent songs).

"Christmas Eve," in "Child's Garden of Song."...... $2.00

"Chinese Narcissus" (a song for Chinese New Year), "Christmas Day," "New Year's Day," "Thanksgiving Day," in "The Cocoa Palm," by Mary Dillingham Frear.

For information in regard to songs for children, write to Mrs. Juliet-Powell Rice, Santa Barbara, Cal., or Prof. Milton A. Lawrence, College Park, Santa Clara county, California.

"Thanksgiving Song," "Christmas Song," "Santa Claus," in "Simple Songs for Little Singers," by Anna B. Tucker.. .50

ENTERTAINMENTS.

"Christmas-tide" (A Tiny Operetta for the Little Ones.) Primary Education Supplement, Nov. '98.

"A Christmas Festival Service," by Nora A. Smith... .25

"Christmas Cantatas."

"At the Court of King Winter," "Christmas Stars" "A Visit from Mother Goose," each.................. .15

Christmas Suggestions.... .... .10

"A Thanksgiving Exercise," "A Xmas Exercise," "The Children's Telegram," "The Christmas Sheaf," "Thanksgiving in Ye Olden Time," "Sufferings and Destiny of the Pilgrims" (Edward Everett), in "Children's Speaker." by John Wesley Hanson, Jr. .... .75

"Christ and the Little Ones," "The Christmas Baby" (Will Carleton)—"The Peerless Speaker."........... .70

"Bud's Christmas Stocking," "Landing of the Pilgrim Fathers" (Felicia Hemans), "Thanksgiving," "Little Nellie's Visit from Santa Claus"—Prescott's "Drawing-room Recitations."

"The Mistletoe Bough" (Illustrated), "A Christmas Exercise," "A Thanksgiving Exercise" (excellent)— "The International Orator," by John Wesley Hanson, Jr. .75

"Christmas Candles".... ...."Popular Educator," Dec., 1897

"Drill of Seasons"..........."Popular Educator," Nov., 1895

"Christmas Exercises"........"Popular Educator," Dec., 1895
"The Popcorn Dance"........"Popular Educator," Nov., 1895
"Mother Goose Entertainment".."Primary School," Dec., 1895
"Christmas Program"..........."Primary School," Dec., 1895

"How to Celebrate Thanksgiving and Christmas in the Schoolroom.".................................... .25
"Recitations for Christmas," by Margaret Holmes.... .25
"Dialogues for Christmas.".......................... .25
"Drills and Marches."............................... .25
"Tableaux, Charades and Pantomimes.".............. .30
"Easy Eentertainments.".............................. .25
Blackboard Stencils ("Xmas Stocking" and "Kriss Kringle").. .05
Pritchard's Choice Dialogues........................ .20
"Tables Turned; or A Christmas for Santa Claus.".... .30
"The Revolt of the Toys.".......................... .20
"Jingle Bells."..................................... .30
"Good Tidings; or, The Sailor-Boys' Christmas.".... .25
"The Day After Christmas" (for two boys and one girl), in "The Teachers' Institute" (Nov., 1893).
"Holiday Selections," by Sarah S. Rice............. .30
"Holiday Entertainments," by Chas. C. Shoemaker.. .30
"Drills and Marches," by E. C. and L. J. Rook...... .25

ENTERTAINMENTS.

"Christmas Eve" (a Pantomime), "A New Year's Address" (Edward Brooks), "Christmas-tide" (three scenes), "Cinderella's Slipper," "To a Christmas Pudding," in "Best Things from Best Authors," by J. W. Shoemaker.

"Epiphany" (Bishop Heber), in "Open Sesame," Vol. I.

"November" (Thomas Hood), "The Christmas Goose at the Cratchits'" (Charles Dickens), "A Christmas Hymn" (Alfred Dommett), "Christmas Carol" (from the Neapolitan), "Christmas Day" (Charles Wesley), in "Open Sesame," Vol. II.

"The Christmas Silence" (Margaret Deland), "Merry Christmas" (Selected), "The Little Pine-Tree" (from the German, Eudora S. Bumstead), in "Nature in Verse," compiled by Mary I. Lovejoy.

"Good Tidings" (From Saint Luke), "While Shepherds Watched Their Flocks by Night" (Nehum Tate), "Christmas Carol" (Old English), "Christmas Bells" (John Keble), "Christmas" (Anonymous), "A Desire" (Adelaide Proctor), "Christmas Carol" (Felicia Hemans), "A Christmas Carol" (Dinah Maria Mulock), "A Christmas Carol" (Christina G. Rossetti), "The Christmas Holly" (Eliza Cook), "Old Christmas" (Mary Howitt), "To the Fir-Tree," "New Year's Eve" (Hans Christian Andersen), "Thanksgiving Day" (Henry Alford), in "Open Sesame," Vol. I.

"The New Christmas" (a one-act drama for three boys and two girls), "The First Christmas Night" (short recitation), "Old Santa Has Struck" (for a girl), "Recitations from the Bible," "The Ten Commandments," in "From Tots to Teens" (January, 1897).

"A Christmas Dialogue" (for one girl and one boy), in "Young Folks' Dialogues," by Chas. C. Shoemaker.... .25

"Thanksgiving" (Charles Follen Adams), in De Witt's "School Speaker."

"Drills and Marches," "Visit of Santa Claus" (for ten boys and eight girls), in "Very Little Dialogues for Very Little Folks;" "Way to Spend Christmas" (three boys and six girls), in Dick's "Little Dialogues;" "Christmas Gifts" (for four little girls), in "School Dialogues" (No. 1, Primary).

RECITATIONS IN "100 CHOICE SELECTIONS."

"The Closing Year" (No. 1).
"Will the New Year Come To-night, Mamma?" (No. 2).
"The Changed Cross" (No. 3).
"A Thanksgiving Sermon" (No. 4).
"Christmas Eve" (No. 9).
"The Pilgrims and the Peas" (No. 11).
"The Puritans" (No. 14).
"Little Rocket's Christmas" (No. 15).
"A Christmas Chant" (No. 16).

"Christmas Night in the Quarters" (No. 16).
"The Christmas Tree" (No. 16).
"The Night After Christmas" (No. 16).
"The Night Before Christmas" (No. 16).
"A Christmas Hymn" (No. 17).
"The Christian's Life" (No. 18).
"The Orphan's Prayer" (No. 19).
"The Christmas Chimes" (No. 20).
"Give Thanks fer What?" (No. 21).
"The Christmas Baby" (No. 22).
"Miltiades Gets the Best of Santa Claus" (No. 23).
"Christ and the Little Ones" (No. 24).
"Consider the Lilies" (No. 24).
"The Lord's Prayer Illustrated" (No. 24).
"The Heart's Charity" (No. 24).
"A Christmas Blessing" (No. 25).

RECITATIONS FOR OLDER PUPILS AND STUDENTS.

Selections from "Ben Hur."
Extracts from Bishop's Simpson's Great "Christmas Sermon."
"Caleb's Courtship" (Thanksgiving Morning). (100 Choice Selections.)
Extracts from Robert Ingersoll's "Christmas Sermon."
"Little John's Christmas" (Whitcomb Riley).
"Ebenezer's Dream" (100 Choice Selections).
"Festive Days,"

A Thanksgiving Speech,
A Thanksgiving Address,
An Exercise Around the Christmas Tree,
A Thanksgiving Song, in "Three-Minute Declamations for
    College Men."...................................$1.00
"The Minuet,"
"The Puritans,"
"A Christmas Camp on the San Gabr'el," in "Three Minute
    Readings for College Girls."
"The Landing of the Pilgrim Fathers," in "American History
    Stories" (Vol. I).

STORIES.

"The Story Hour," Kate Douglas Wiggin............ $1.00
"In the Child's World," Emilie Poulsson............ 2.00
"Kindergarten Stories and Morning Talks," Sarah E.
    Wiltse.. .75
"St. Nicholas" (Nov. and Dec. numbers, also March, '95).
"Wide Awake."
"Babyland."
"Youth's Companion."
"Old Father Christmas" (Mrs. Ewing).
"A Santa Claus Story," "Child Stories and Rhymes," by
    Emilie Poulsson............................... $1.40
"The Bird's Christmas Carol," Kate Douglas Wiggin.
"Puritans and Pilgrims," in "American History Stories"
    (Vol. I).

"Christmas Eve"................ ....5c. Classics
"Story of the Pilgrims".................. ....5c. Classics
"Stories of Colonial Children," by Mara L. Pratt,......
....Boards, 40c; Cloth, 60c.
"Evergreens" (Christmas) in "All the Year Round (Winter)."

For songs, poems, stories, pictures, and suggestions, see November and December numbers of "The Plan Book."

SUGGESTIONS FOR CHRISTMAS DECORATIONS.

Send two-cent stamp for catalogue to the Perry Picture Company, Malden, Mass.

Christmas Stencils.

Stencils for Blackboards (200 or more designs, each 5c.).

For pictures, see November and December numbers of "Babyland," "Wide Awake," "Saint Nicholas," "Youth's Companion," and "Ladies' Home Journal."

See also Emilie Poulsson's "Finger-plays," and "The Child's Garden of Song."

Have pupils copy short Christmas poems and prose selections, also proverbs and appropriate verses from the Bible.

MANUAL TRAINING.

Have pupils string seeds gathered during the fall.

Box covers, picture frames, et cetera, may be decorated with designs of shells or seeds.

Have pupils paint and draw from the object, toyon, holly, mistletoe, pepper, yerba buena, etc.

Teach children to make and decorate in water colors, picture frames, book covers, pen wipers, book markers, glove and handkerchief boxes, blotters, calendars, etc.

Fold Christmas stars, using yellow, gold, or silver paper.

Weave mats, book markers, fans, baskets, glove, collar and handkerchief boxes, etc.

Teach freehand weaving, using strips of paper, ribbon, straw, twine, thread, bamboo, willow, etc.

Teach pupils to model paper weights and other articles in clay and wax.

Teach girls to outline on cardboard, doilies, etc.; make needle-books, pin-balls, pen wipers, canvas mats (ornamented with criss-cross stitch), work bags (outlining initial letter), pin flats, paper dolls (dressed for historic effect), holders, splashers, umbrella cases, cane cases, hair receivers, "ladies' companions," "bachelor comforts," linen or denim pillows; embroider linen picture frames, book covers, etc.; dress dolls, and make complete dolls' outfits; articles of clothing for poor children, etc.

Teach boys to make useful household articles; also, toy wagons, wheelbarrows, dolls' houses, etc.

For slojd books and slojd material, send to the publishers of this book. Send for Larsson's Working Drawings in Slojd."

NOTE.

All of the entertainment, recitation, dialogue, and other books, blackboard stencils, songs, aids, material, etc., mentioned in this book can be obtained from

THE WHITAKER & RAY COMPANY,
723 Market St., San Francisco, Cal.

Complete descriptive price lists, circulars, etc., will be sent on application.

www.ingramcontent.com/pod-product-compliance
Lightning Source LLC
Chambersburg PA
CBHW021728220426
43662CB00008B/752